Refreshingly, this text stays focused on the actual behavior of intercultural communication. While it uses many contrasts to the Japanese cultural style, the four dimensions of competence it illustrates are generally applicable to the intentional development of *global competence* in language classrooms and international exchange. And in arguing for 'adopting values beyond our horizon,' it appropriately treats cultural values as preferences for certain kinds of behavior, making it easier for readers to avoid ethical dualities and instead increase their range of suitable communication.

Milton J. Bennett, Ph.D., Executive Director, Intercultural Development Research Institute

In 2015, nearly 200 United Nations (UN) member states adopted the UN Sustainable Development Goals and their targets to improve life on our shared planet by 2030. The fourth goal calls for quality education for all and addresses two key areas: global citizenship and sustainable development. In 2009, I also acknowledged a similar goal in an article titled "Developing Intercultural Competencies: An Educational Imperative for the 21st Century." The current work by Egitim and Harumi now makes an important contribution toward advancing these goals by providing a pedagogical model that may be applied cross-culturally in classroom settings. This is a work that should be in the hands of all educators and students involved in language and cross-cultural education.

Alvino E. Fantini, Ph.D., Professor Emeritus School for International Training, Brattleboro, Vermont, USA

Soyhan Egitim and Seiko Harumi's *Developing Global Competence in World Language Education: A Four-Step Framework for Success* presents a convincing challenge to rethink language education beyond proficiency and test performance. Their Four-Step Framework provides a compelling model for integrating linguistic proficiency, cross-cultural knowledge, adaptability, and intercultural values into second language learning. By emphasizing curiosity, communication flexibility, and reflective practice, the book moves language education toward promoting globally competent speakers who can navigate real-world intercultural interactions. The book is essential reading for language educators, curriculum designers, and policymakers seeking to bridge the gap between policy aspirations and classroom realities. Graduate students in applied linguistics and intercultural communication will also find its insights invaluable. With practical applications grounded in empirical studies, this work provides the necessary tools to cultivate language learners who are not just proficient but also culturally and communicatively agile in a globalized world.

Jim McKinley, Ph.D., Professor of Applied Linguistics,
University College London

For Product Safety Concerns and Information please contact our EU representative GPSR@taylorandfrancis.com
Taylor & Francis Verlag GmbH, Kaufingerstraße 24, 80331 München, Germany

www.ingramcontent.com/pod-product-compliance
Lightning Source LLC
Chambersburg PA
CBHW061714300426
44115CB00014B/2686

inclusive communication 86
interactional competence (IC) 34–5, 38
intercultural competence 4, 7–9, 11, 13–14, 138–9
intercultural communicative competence (ICC) 10, 13, 43
intercultural conflict 88–91
intercultural education 28–9, 31, 46, 56–7
intercultural flexibility 67, 72, 81
intercultural language education 28, 46, 56
intercultural repertoire 21–2, 70
internal conflict 99–100

Japan Association of Language Teachers (JALT) 53

Kao wo Tateru (saving face) 77
Kuki wo Yomu (reading the air) 77

Leaderful Classroom Practices Framework 47–8
Lingua Franca 5, 9
listening intently 19, 73
low-context cultures 89

majority-group/minority-group dynamics 87
media influences 99
meta-pragmatic focus 54
Ministry of Education, Culture, Sports, Science and Technology (MEXT) 5

native speakerism 9–10, 32–3
Navigate Cross-Cultural Conflict 96
near-peer role models (NPRMs) 33, 49, 52
non-verbal cues 67, 70–1, 79

Organization for Economic Cooperation and Development (OECD) 2–3

peer feedback 75–6
post-colonial societies 90
power dynamics 90
practical training 71–2
pragmatic awareness 44
pragmatic competence 34, 56
pragmatic failure 112–14
pragmatics 33–7, 53, 106, 113, 165
Pragmatics Special Interest Group (SIG) 53

Recognize New Values 96
reflective practice 97–8, 100–1, 72

self-compassion 100
shuttle bus analogy 68
silence in communication 78
social acceptance 173, 177–80
social exclusion 88, 95
sources of intercultural conflict 88–90
speech acts 34, 53–4
steps to integrating values beyond our horizon 96–7
study abroad 13, 20, 44, 51, 87, 89, 95, 109–10, 122–8, 134–6, 181–6

tandem learning 133–4, 136–41, 160, 162–9, 186
Test of English for International Communication (TOEIC) 15, 31
turn-taking 35–6, 57, 108, 106, 136, 141, 150, 162–3

universal communicators 8
universally acceptable communication style 70–1
United Nations Educational, Scientific and Cultural Organization (UNESCO) 2–3

Wa (harmony) 77
Western, Educated, Industrialized, Religious, and Democratic societies (WEIRD) 11, 40, 50, 67, 69, 71, 73, 78, 81, 86, 95

Developing Global Competence in World Language Education

This book presents a four-step framework to help English as a world language (EWL) learners successfully develop global competence, which is defined as the skills, values, and behaviors that prepare young people to thrive in diverse environments. The book showcases practical methods and strategies supported by autoethnography and empirical studies to detail the four elements of the framework towards developing global competence: English language proficiency, cross-cultural knowledge, adopting flexibility in oral communication, and embracing values beyond our horizons. While the English language and culture provide essential input for effective communication, developing flexibility in communication styles and viewing conflict as an opportunity for growth can help L2 learners navigate intercultural encounters more effectively and achieve cross-cultural adaptation. This text will be beneficial to language learners, intercultural communication majors, researchers, and educators in TESOL/EFL/ESL programs, as well as in-service teachers of English language learners (ELLs).

Soyhan Egitim, EdD, has lived and worked in multicultural societies, including Turkey, where he is originally from, Canada, and Japan. Currently, he serves as an associate professor in the Faculty of Global and Regional Studies at Toyo University, where he teaches English language courses and global competence seminars.

Seiko Harumi, PhD, has lived and worked in Japan and the UK as a second/foreign language teacher of English and Japanese and an academic at secondary and tertiary levels. She is currently a Senior Lecturer in Japanese and Applied Linguistics (Education) at the School of Oriental and African Studies (SOAS), University of London, where she teaches Japanese language courses.

Developing Global Competence in World Language Education

A Four-Step Framework for Success

Soyhan Egitim and Seiko Harumi

Routledge
Taylor & Francis Group
NEW YORK AND LONDON

Designed cover image: © Routledge

First published 2026
by Routledge
605 Third Avenue, New York, NY 10158

and by Routledge
4 Park Square, Milton Park, Abingdon, Oxon, OX14 4RN

Routledge is an imprint of the Taylor & Francis Group, an informa business

© 2026 Soyhan Egitim and Seiko Harumi

The right of Soyhan Egitim and Seiko Harumi to be identified as authors of this work has been asserted in accordance with sections 77 and 78 of the Copyright, Designs and Patents Act 1988.

All rights reserved. No part of this book may be reprinted or reproduced or utilised in any form or by any electronic, mechanical, or other means, now known or hereafter invented, including photocopying and recording, or in any information storage or retrieval system, without permission in writing from the publishers.

Trademark notice: Product or corporate names may be trademarks or registered trademarks, and are used only for identification and explanation without intent to infringe.

ISBN: 9781032814360 (hbk)
ISBN: 9781032814346 (pbk)
ISBN: 9781003499848 (ebk)

DOI: 10.4324/9781003499848

Typeset in Palatino
by Newgen Publishing UK

Contents

Preface xi
Soyhan Egitim xi
Seiko Harumi xiv

1 **Introduction to Four-Step Framework for**
  Global Competence 1
  1.1 *Defining* Global Competence 1
  1.2 *English Language Education and* Global Competence
      in the Asia-Pacific Region 5
  1.3 *The Evolving Concept of Intercultural Competence* 8
  1.4 *Introduction to the* Global Competence *Framework* 14

2 **Intercultural Language Education: Treating**
  Language and Culture as One 28
  2.1 *The Perception of Intercultural Education in the*
      Asia-Pacific Region 28
  2.2 *Challenges and Opportunities of Integrating Intercultural*
      Education into English as a World Language
      Curriculum 30
  2.3 *Pragmatic Perspectives on L2 Use* 33
  2.4 *Cultivating Cross-Cultural Understanding Through*
      Intercultural Encounters 39
  2.5 *Facilitating L2 Interaction in Diverse Socio-Cultural*
      Contexts 42
  2.6 *Intercultural Language Education Through* Leaderful
      Classroom *Practices* 46
  2.7 *Near-Peer Role Models as Collaborative Leaders* 49
  2.8 *Leaderful Intercultural Classroom Activities in*
      English Language Classes 53
  2.9 *Conclusion* 56

3 **Adaptability in Communication Styles: Balancing Assertiveness and Subtlety** 66
   3.1 *Balancing Assertiveness and Subtlety in Intercultural Exchanges 66*
   3.2 *Exploring Communication Styles Across Cultures: Why Do We Communicate the Way We Do? 68*
   3.3 *Developing a Universally Acceptable Communication Style: Is it Feasible? 70*
   3.4 *Balancing Communication Styles Through Intercultural Flexibility 72*
   3.5 *Conclusion 80*

4 **From Conflict to Mutuality: Adopting Values Beyond Our Horizon** 86
   4.1 *Beyond Ethnocentrism: Understanding Cultural Fluidity and Inclusive Communication 86*
   4.2 *The Role of Conflict in Intercultural Interactions 88*
      4.2.1 *Understanding the Sources of Intercultural Conflict 88*
      4.2.2 *Impact of Conflict on Intercultural Relationships 91*
   4.3 *Learning New Values Through Conflict-Resolution Dynamics 93*
   4.4 *Steps to Integrating Values Beyond Our Horizon 96*
      4.4.1 *Balancing Cultural Identity and Newly Acquired Values 98*
   4.5 *Conclusion 101*

5 **Developing *Global Competence* Through Self and Collaborative Reflections** 105
   5.1 *Applying a* Global Competence *Framework to Intercultural Interactions 105*
      5.1.1 *Global Perspectives on Intercultural Interactions 106*
      5.1.2 *Cross-Cultural Problematic Encounters of Seiko Harumi 109*

5.2 The Use of Silence in English Language Classrooms in Japan 115
    5.2.1 Case study 1: Silence in the L2 Classroom 116
    5.2.2 Case Study 2: Study Abroad Contexts and Communication with International Students 122
5.3 Conclusion 129

6 Pedagogical Insights for Enhancing Global Competence in the Classroom and Beyond 133

6.1 East Asian Learners' Study Abroad Experiences and Tandem Learning 133
6.2 Practical Applications of Global Competence Development 141
    6.2.1 Intercultural Interaction Between Japanese English Language Learners and Japanese Language Learners in the UK 142
    6.2.2 Lessons in Intercultural Communication: Perspectives from Multiple Voices 147
    6.2.3 Benefits, Challenges, and Future Possibilities 160
    6.2.4 Language and Culture Exchange Program 162
6.3 Cross-Cultural Encounters of English and Japanese Language Learners Studying Abroad 169
    6.3.1 English Language Learners 169
    6.3.2 Japanese Language Learners 173
6.4 Reflections on L2 Learners' Study Abroad Experiences 181
    6.4.1 Practical Approaches to Promoting Intercultural Communication on Campus 181
    6.4.2 Cultural Immersion Events 182
    6.4.3 Intercultural Workshops 183
    6.4.4 Intercultural Sports Day 184
6.5 Conclusion 186

Index   192

Preface

Soyhan Egitim

In today's globalized world, the ability to navigate cultural boundaries has become an essential skill for success. Engaging with people from diverse linguistic, cultural, and social backgrounds demands not only language proficiency but also an understanding of cultural nuances, empathy, and adaptability. This book aims to meet these needs by offering a comprehensive framework for fostering *global competence*—a set of skills that transcends borders and prepares both students and educators to thrive in multicultural environments.

In our *global competence* framework, we emphasize four essential steps: linguistic proficiency, cross-cultural knowledge, adaptability in communication styles, and the willingness to embrace new values—even those that extend beyond our horizon. This book explores these four key components as part of a broader *global competence* framework, aimed at providing students with the skills and attitudes necessary to thrive in our interconnected world. Our framework is not merely theoretical but is grounded in thorough empirical research and the practical experience of educators and students who have engaged with diverse cultural contexts.

Needless to say, the English language, as the global Lingua Franca, plays a pivotal role in intercultural communication as people from various linguistic and cultural backgrounds use English as their common language in their daily interactions across the globe. Through the lens of world language education, we emphasize the significance of English as a valuable tool for communication despite the challenges involved in aligning educational policies with classroom realities. While English language education is essential, true *global competence* extends far beyond language proficiency. It involves understanding the diverse perspectives and worldviews of others in cross-cultural interactions. Our framework emphasizes that cultivating curiosity about other cultures is most meaningful when it is done through genuine intercultural interactions. As our curiosity grows, so does our motivation to learn more about others and deepen our cross-cultural understanding.

The third step involves gaining the ability to adapt to different communication styles. It is unrealistic to expect that a universally acceptable communication style can be fully achieved. However, our framework emphasizes that it is possible to develop cognitive flexibility to adapt to different communication styles according to the cultural context we are in. This step includes two key categories: assertive communication for students from implicit contexts and implicit communication for students from assertive contexts. Our goal is not to abandon one style for another but to develop the ability to flexibly switch between them depending on the situation. This way, we can "board the bus" of intercultural interactions and "get off at any point," while navigating diverse cultural contexts.

Moreover, cultural adaptation is a continuous and evolving process, in which we believe the focus should be on supporting individuals to maintain their cultural values, beliefs, and practices, while embracing new perspectives. However, adopting new values is not a linear process; it involves raising awareness of the different phases individuals may experience. Through intercultural contact and reflective practice, we can develop cognitive flexibility to thrive in unfamiliar cultural environments. The final step of our framework, outlined—*Navigating Cross-Cultural Conflict, Recognizing New Values, Acknowledging Differences Through Reflection*, and *Adding New Values to Our Intercultural Repertoire*—provides a dynamic approach to incorporating new values while maintaining our cultural integrity.

However, it is unrealistic to expect that we can adopt new values without experiencing conflict. In fact, we may need to treat conflict as a natural part of intercultural encounters, as it brings opportunities to develop empathy, tolerance, and acceptance toward others. By reframing conflict in this way, we can open the door to deeper reflection, and understanding, which would lead to meaningful cross-cultural relationships. By transcending ethnocentric views, we can gradually integrate new values into our cultural framework and develop the cognitive flexibility needed to adapt to diverse environments.

As a final note, we would like to emphasize that our insights are not merely theoretical; they are deeply informed by our own journeys of navigating cultural differences and adapting to new environments. Our diverse yet complementary experiences of living and working in different cross-cultural settings, as well as our ongoing need to adapt to various cultural contexts, have been central to shaping these insights. Having lived in Japan for nearly two decades, I gained proficiency in the Japanese language and learned to navigate the implicit communication styles commonly used here. Conflict and resolution have always been a natural part of my daily interactions. My classroom experiences and challenges have further underscored the need for a comprehensive approach, one that integrates *language*, *culture*, *attitudes*, and *values* through a systematic framework to guide educators and students through the steps required to become globally competent citizens. Together, these components have shaped the foundation upon which this book is built.

Finally, I would like to share a few words about my co-author, Seiko Harumi. From the very beginning of this project, Seiko and I have worked together in great harmony, all while balancing the demands of work and family responsibilities. Her diverse yet complementary experiences to mine have enriched our understanding of the complexities of cross-cultural interactions, allowing us to develop a more comprehensive and well-rounded approach to the concepts explored in this book. We hope that our *global competence* framework will provide both students and educators with a practical tool to navigate intercultural challenges and foster a deeper appreciation of diverse perspectives in our increasingly interconnected world.

Seiko Harumi

Over the past few years since the global pandemic, language learning and teaching environments have changed dramatically. This transitional phase brought us an accelerated digital era, enabling second language learners to communicate more easily with L1 speakers of their target language or other language learners across different sociocultural contexts, virtually and globally. While this technology opened new doors for diverse educational approaches, both for learners and educators, the significant role that *global competence* plays was even further intensified for language learners who needed to deal with various interactional demands and experience curiosity in intercultural contexts. These circumstances naturally led them to encounter situations in which they needed to: (1) be equipped with necessary interactional and cultural repertoires; (2) be able to maintain interaction for co-construction of intercultural dialogues; (3) understand others' cultural practices; (4) adopt new communicative styles taking account of others' socio-cultural backgrounds and also (5) embrace fresh cultural and interactional values during cross-cultural interaction. Our book's core framework intends to introduce such steps for learners of a wide range of second languages from diverse cultures.

In this book, English language Education, specifically in Japanese English as a world language context extending to Asia-Pacific regions, is the key focus in our discussion of current educational practices. Nevertheless, we also explored ways Japanese learners' communication styles and values are understood by learners of Japanese languages in multilingual contexts, including exchange students in Japan, and we incorporated their voices as expressed in empirical studies and educational practices which highlighted diversity in the understanding of Japanese and English cultural and interactional repertoires. The multiple voices of these learners, which stemmed from diverse perspectives, provided significant insights into the ways in which we, as educators, can see the values of intercultural communication and guide learners of second languages from every part of the world. Although our book focuses on Japan and other parts of the Asia-Pacific region, it highlights a pedagogical framework which embraces ways in which both learners and educators can broaden perspectives on intercultural communication within diverse cultural contexts from multiple points of view.

As a former learner of English as a second language who grew up in Japan and also taught English there as a non-native English speaker, I share Japanese English language learners' intercultural communication struggles, which involve tackling invisible interactional rules and ways in which communication styles are evaluated while practicing self-identity as a sign of active agency. On the other hand, as somebody who has lived in the UK for more than two decades, teaching Japanese language to non-Japanese students, I have enjoyed invaluable opportunities to see how Japanese language and cultures are interpreted from the perspectives of my students, and their insights became an invaluable learning resource for me as an educator.

As a final note, I would also like to mention my co-author, Soyhan Egitim, with whom I shared our cross-cultural talk, even before the start of our project. Soyhan's invaluable and diverse cultural experiences, in many countries, were a great source of inspiration for this book project, in which we were able to examine multiple educational practices, adopting our core framework in diverse contexts. We hope that learners and teachers of various world languages can gain insights from this book and also join us in our journey through the world of intercultural interaction and dialogue.

Introduction to Four-Step Framework for *Global Competence*

Soyhan Egitim and Seiko Harumi

1.1 Defining *Global Competence*

We live in an era that is more interconnected and interdependent than ever before. With increasing global mobility, the ability to understand and value diverse perspectives, as well as to engage in open and effective interactions with people from different cultures, has become indispensable. Digital transformation, the expansion of global supply chains, and the growth of the global start-up ecosystem have further highlighted the need for globally competent individuals. Organizations now seek professionals with a broad range of skills and attitudes to navigate the complexities and opportunities of our rapidly evolving world. In this context, *global competence* has emerged as a key term to encompass the skills and attitudes required to thrive in an increasingly interconnected and dynamic global landscape.

Global competence embodies cross-cultural awareness, an understanding of global dynamics, social responsibility, and a holistic appreciation of global interconnectedness (Mansilla

& Gardner, 2007). Over the past few decades, its definition has evolved to reflect the growing complexities of our interconnected world. Hanvey defined *global competence* as the ability to cultivate a collective consciousness that embraces our shared humanity on a global scale (as cited in Smith & Luce, 1979). This marked the first significant emphasis on sustainability and social responsibility within the concept.

Nearly three decades later, Mansilla and Gardner (2007) expanded the definition, emphasizing the importance of fostering global consciousness to develop a deeper understanding of our interconnected world. This perspective placed a strong focus on awareness as a cornerstone of *global competence*. Reimers (2009) further refined the concept, proposing a contemporary framework that incorporates multiple dimensions. These include *perspective consciousness*, the understanding that individual viewpoints are not universally shared; *state-of-the-planet awareness*, which reflects knowledge of global environmental and societal conditions; *cross-cultural understanding*, involving the recognition and appreciation of cultural diversity; *knowledge of global dynamics*, highlighting the interconnectedness of global systems; and *awareness of human choices*, emphasizing the impact of individual and collective decisions on global outcomes. Together, these evolving definitions underscore the importance of *global competence* as a vital skill set for navigating and thriving in an increasingly complex and interconnected world.

As we entered the last few decades, the definitions became more complex and reflective of the current dynamics. The Organization for Economic Cooperation and Development (OECD) provided the most widely recognized definition of *global competence*: "the capacity to examine local, global and intercultural issues, to understand and appreciate the perspectives and world views of others, to engage in open, appropriate, and effective interactions with people from different cultures, and to act for collective well-being and sustainable development (OECD, 2018, p. 4)." The definition by the OECD captures the dynamic and ever-evolving nature of *global competence*. In tandem with the OECD definition, UNESCO introduced the global citizenship education framework to foster students' understanding of global dynamics, and a collective mindset to solve universal problems, while acting effectively and responsibly at local, national, and global levels for a more peaceful and sustainable world (Engel et al., 2019, p. 121). UNESCO's framing of *global competence* education provided the first direction for higher education institutions around the world. A growing number of institutions across the globe have incorporated elements of *global competence* education to foster global human resources, who can tackle the existing and emerging global challenges while harnessing the opportunities our interconnected world has to offer (Engel et al., 2019).

As highlighted in the OECD (2018) definition, one of the first steps toward becoming a globally competent citizen is achieving sufficient linguistic competence in the English language. This enables individuals to "understand and appreciate the perspectives and world views of others and engage in open, appropriate, and effective intercultural interactions" (p. 4). In many regions worldwide, including the Asia-Pacific, high proficiency in English is regarded as a crucial element of *global competence*. This is largely due to its widespread use across diverse fields such as education, business, politics, economics, social sciences, and technology (Meng et al., 2018; Sakamoto & Rogers, 2023).

The English language serves as a common communication tool across various industries in the world. Many organizations recognize that diversity infuses creativity and innovation. People from different backgrounds bring varied perspectives. They may see problems from angles others might miss. This dynamic often challenges conventional thinking, which may otherwise echo existing norms. Individuals on diverse teams also navigate the complexity of adapting to different customs and mindsets. The constraints and adversities facing them along the way may spark innovative solutions. The English language is what enables diverse teams to understand and appreciate the perspectives of others as they navigate the complexity of intercultural interactions.

Another critical component highlighted in the definitions is cross-cultural understanding (Mansilla & Gardner, 2007; OECD, 2018; Reimers, 2009). This ability helps individuals comprehend and value the perspectives and worldviews of others in cross-cultural interactions. There is more than one way to gain cross-cultural understanding, yet ambiguity remains about how one can develop this skill in a meaningful way. Cultivating curiosity about other cultures is often the first step toward cross-cultural understanding (Mikhailov, 2016). Research suggests that one of the most effective ways to foster cultural curiosity is through intercultural contact (Bennett, 2013; Bennett, 2023; Houghton, 2014). While there are various approaches to nurturing this curiosity, intercultural contact with people from different cultural backgrounds is effective in sparking greater curiosity and, in turn, promoting more knowledge acquisition.

In the past, intercultural researchers emphasized openness as a key component in integrating intercultural learning into various frameworks (Byram, 1997, 2009; Deardorff, 2006; Fantini, 2018). However, while openness is important, it is difficult to imagine anyone developing curiosity about other cultures without engaging in genuine intercultural contact. If we acquire information solely from books or other materials, we may satisfy our curiosity, but our attempt will likely stop there due to the one-dimensional nature of this type of knowledge acquisition.

Recent research emphasizes the dynamic and reciprocal nature of this process (Egitim, 2024; Houghton, 2014; Mikhailov, 2016). In other words, meaningful intercultural contact raises individuals' curiosity, and in turn, curiosity should lead to the desire to engage in further intercultural contact. This dynamic and reciprocal process facilitates cross-cultural knowledge acquisition. Furthermore, globalization has transformed higher education through the widening global academic network. The increasing competition and cooperation in education and research necessitated the integration of *global competence* education into school curricula. Therefore, many institutions, particularly in the Asia-Pacific region, transformed educational strategies to equip students with the necessary skills and attitudes to thrive in global environments (Hofmeyr, 2023; Meng et al., 2018; Sakamoto & Rogers, 2023). International curricula, global exchange programs, and global cooperation initiatives were adopted to develop students' communication skills, cross-cultural understanding, and collective consciousness.

Over the last couple of decades, Governments also promoted the internationalization of universities through competitive funding programs such as the *Top Global University* initiative of the Japanese government, the Korean government's efforts in promoting global responsibility through inbound mobility and integration of the Sustainable Development Goals (SDGs), and the new initiatives by the Chinese government to promote offshore programs, collaborative research opportunities, and study abroad and talent mobility initiatives (Jon & Yoo, 2021; Yamada, 2021; Zheng & Kapoor, 2021). All these efforts are made to remain competitive by enhancing cooperation in education and research globally in the ever-changing global higher education landscape.

1.2 English Language Education and *Global Competence* in the Asia-Pacific Region

English, as the world's Lingua Franca, is the most widely used language for facilitating cross-cultural communication globally. Proficiency in English is widely recognized as a critical component of global citizenship, as it enables individuals to connect with people from diverse backgrounds, acquire cross-cultural knowledge, and foster collaborations across cultures (Davidson & Liu, 2020; Estellés & Fischman, 2021). Consequently, English language education has become a central focus of *global competence* initiatives in the Asia-Pacific region (Hofmeyr, 2023; Kubota & Takeda, 2021).

Since 2011, the Ministry of Education, Culture, Sports, Science and Technology (MEXT) has reformed English language education with the aim of fostering global human resources, also referred to as *Global Jinzai* in the Japanese language (Hofmeyr, 2023). As indicated in the definition provided by the MEXT, high language proficiency, and communication competence were particularly emphasized:

> *Those who are rooted in their identity as Japanese by an in-depth understanding of the Japanese culture and can thrive in a variety of fields with (a) high levels of language ability and communication competence, (b) autonomy and proactiveness, and (c) a spirit of intercultural understanding* (Kubota & Takeda, 2021, p. 466).

Furthermore, higher education institutions ramped up their internationalization efforts through international faculty expansion, study abroad initiatives for domestic students, and international student exchange programs with the hope that these reforms would also enhance the quality of English language education (Hofmeyr, 2023; Kubota & Takeda, 2021). However, as it stands, the current policies do not appear to provide teachers and students with clear guidelines for how they should accomplish what is expected of them in terms of becoming a *Global Jinzai* (Hofmeyr, 2023). Furthermore, the policies tend to treat English language and intercultural communication as two separate entities (Egitim & Sandu, 2023; Fritz & Sandu, 2020), even though opportunities for Japanese people to engage in intercultural interactions mainly involve using the English language (Shaules, 2019). Consequently, a disconnect remains between policy expectations and classroom realities. While students may achieve high test scores and acquire cross-cultural knowledge, they often struggle to navigate real-world conflicts arising from intercultural encounters (Egitim, 2022a; Egitim, 2024).

On the other hand, Confucian-oriented learning is deep-rooted in the Asia-Pacific region, which relies on rote memorization and exam performance in all subjects, including English language education (Egitim, 2021; Richter, 2022; Zhang & Bournot-Trites, 2021). Confucianist norms emphasize implicit communication, collective identity, harmony, and consensus-building (Matsuyama et al., 2019; Richter, 2022; Zhang & Bournot-Trites, 2021). There is usually a hierarchical relationship between the teacher and students to maintain these norms in the classroom. In this dynamic, the teacher is viewed as the ultimate knowledge source while students act as passive recipients expecting to be spoon-fed new knowledge (Egitim, 2021). This style of education can be effective in "completing fixed tasks, maintaining consistency, productivity, and precision as in the case of machines," yet it may fall short of addressing the needs emphasized in the *Global Jinzai* description, such as critical thinking, creativity, and global awareness through interactive learning.

Furthermore, research shows that there is a lack of self-esteem in local language teachers' English language proficiency (Egitim, 2022c; Steele & Zhang, 2016), which could lead to classes taught in students' first language (L1) as the medium of instruction with heavy reliance on textbooks. On the other hand, there appears to be a gap in English as a world language (EWL) teachers' (used instead of foreign language) interpretation of students' needs and expectations and the realities of language classrooms. For instance, engaging in self-expression in front of others may be viewed as a difficult task or at best, an unnecessary attempt for many Japanese students as they may find themselves in situations where they confront the values they were raised with, such as "groupism, harmony, and avoidance of confrontation" (Egitim, 2022b, p. 307). Despite these challenges, many higher education institutions in the Asia-Pacific region continue to reform their English language curricula by including components of *global competence* education through active learning tools (Galloway et al., 2020).

While English language education is essential, achieving *global competence* requires more than language proficiency. It involves understanding diverse perspectives, critically analyzing global issues, and fostering a collective consciousness to address shared challenges on a global scale. Developing this collective consciousness and appreciating diverse perspectives necessitates enhancing students' intercultural competence, which we regard as a cornerstone of global citizenship education. In the following section, we present a comprehensive discussion of intercultural competence, including various frameworks that outline its key components.

1.3 The Evolving Concept of Intercultural Competence

One of the first questions was posed by Gardner (1962) to show the significance of cross-cultural communication, "To what degree is it actually possible, for an expert from one culture to communicate with, to get through to, persons of another culture?" (as cited in Rathje, 2007, p. 254). With this question, Gardner (1962) founded the concept of "universal communicators" who possessed certain characteristics, including "integrity, stability, extroversion, socialization in universal values" along with "special intuitive, and telepathic abilities" which helped them successfully navigate intercultural encounters (as cited in Rathje, 2007, p. 254). Over the decades, numerous other attempts have been made to offer a universally accepted definition of intercultural competence. Thomas et al. (2010) defined intercultural competence as "the ability to shape the process of intercultural interaction in a way that avoids or contextualizes misunderstandings while creating opportunities for cooperative problem-solving that is acceptable and productive for all involved" (p. 141). In contrast, Bennett (2013) highlighted sensitivity, openness, and adaptability as key traits of intercultural competence, essential for supporting effective and appropriate interactions across cultural boundaries.

Despite the numerous definitions offered by scholars, defining the continuously evolving and dynamic phenomenon of intercultural competence was challenging enough due to its multifaceted nature and context-dependent features. Therefore, Deardorff (2006) took a different approach and performed a study to understand the most agreed-upon components of intercultural competence, premised on 23 intercultural experts' perspectives. Based on this study, the most widely agreed-upon definition of intercultural competence was "the ability to communicate effectively and appropriately in intercultural situations based on one's cross-cultural knowledge, skills, and attitudes," while the only component receiving a consensus from all 23 experts was "the understanding of others' world views" (Deardorff, 2006, pp. 247–248), which is commonly considered the hardest competency to develop.

The definition of intercultural competence remains elusive due to its multifaceted, context-dependent, and ever-evolving nature. Intercultural competence requires continuous learning and openness to diverse perspectives (Deardorff, 2009; Fantini, 2018; Holliday, 2021). As the most widely agreed-upon definition indicates, intercultural competence goes beyond language proficiency and cross-cultural knowledge (Deardorff, 2006). Empathy, curiosity, and respect for different world views and values, as well as flexibility and adaptability to new circumstances, remain critical in our interconnected world (Egitim, 2022a; Egitim & Sandu, 2023).

During this endeavor, language plays a fundamental role as a bridge to understanding different cultural contexts during intercultural encounters. On the other hand, intercultural communication is not just about words; it encompasses nuances, nonverbal cues, and cultural norms associated with language use. In other words, language facilitates communication, and intercultural competence ensures effective interactions across cultural boundaries, forming an intertwined and interconnected relationship between the two.

The English language, as the global Lingua Franca, plays a pivotal role in intercultural communication as people from various linguistic and cultural backgrounds use English as their common language in their daily interactions across the globe. Until the early 90s, the goals of English language education had been centered around the belief that native speakers of the English language were ideal language teachers due to their presumably superior linguistic competence. Holliday (2006) described this model as a "divisive force which originates within particular educational cultures of the English-speaking West" (p. 385). Researchers also attempted to capture inequality and discrimination associated with the concept of native speakerism (Egitim, 2022a; Lowe & Pinner, 2016; Maganaka, 2023). Other issues raised with this model include the homogeneity assumption, which suggests that all native speakers share the same linguistic competence (Holliday, 2006; Wilkinson, 2020), power imbalance which indicates that native speakers are often considered more authoritative, leading to unequal power relations between them and non-native speakers (Holliday, 2006; Lowe & Pinner, 2016). Cultural bias perpetuated by native speakerism, which favors Western norms and values (Houghton & Rivers, 2013; Lowe & Pinner, 2016), impacts recruitment policies, as institutions may prioritize hiring native speakers while sometimes overlooking qualified non-native teachers (Egitim, 2022a; Maganaka, 2023).

Considering all these deficiencies of the model, efforts were made towards a more inclusive approach that values diverse language backgrounds and intercultural competence. Byram's (1997) intercultural speaker concept was one of the first examples of this movement in world language (used instead of foreign language) research. The model describes the ideal language learner as an individual who has "the ability to interact with others with different cultural values and perspectives, mediate between those different perspectives, and have the consciousness of their differences" (p. 5). The model emphasized the "educational" value of world language learning beyond linguistic conventions and encouraged learners to see themselves as "intercultural citizens" who bridge cultural differences for the common good (Byram, 2009, p. 322).

The intercultural speaker possesses several attributes:

Attitudes and Values: An intercultural speaker adopts a curious and open mindset, critically examining their own values, beliefs, and behaviors instead of assuming that their perspective is the only correct one. They are capable of decentering—viewing their worldview from an outsider's lens.

Mediation Skills: The intercultural speaker acts as a mediator, bridging different cultural understandings. They facilitate dialogue and enable joint actions that contribute to societal improvement.

Intercultural Communicative Competence (ICC): This model offers a theoretical framework for educators to develop the necessary knowledge, skills, and attitudes for positive intercultural engagement within and beyond language education. Key components of the model include linguistic competence (proficiency in the target language), sociocultural competence (understanding cultural norms, values, and practices of others), and intercultural competence (the ability to navigate cultural differences and adapt behavior) (Byram, 1997, p. 34).

Byram's model provided valuable insights into intercultural competence, yet it also received its fair share of critiques from the research community. In theory, the model appears to be equipped with ideal features to demonstrate intercultural competence, yet it appears to neglect the complexities inherent in intercultural interactions. Since all intercultural interactions are dialogic and relational, developing intercultural competence requires a multidimensional approach emphasizing the relational and dialogic aspects of such encounters (Holliday, 2021; Moon, 2023; Noels et al., 2020). For instance, receptiveness and curiosity may be viewed as valuable competencies in Western, Educated, Industrialized, Religious, and Democratic (WEIRD) societies, but in some other contexts, where silence and subtlety are viewed as a form of self-expression, openness may not be viewed as essential (Harumi, 2011).

Furthermore, questions were also raised about the model's feasibility and fit. While it is idealistic to think that language learners would progress toward the intercultural speaker status through formal education, including culture-based tasks in language classrooms and residence abroad experiences, the inherently complex nature of intercultural encounters makes the practical application a challenge. Cultural differences, language barriers, implicit rules, stereotypes and prejudices, power dynamics, emotional complexities, individual differences, and other contextual factors create a complex dynamic, which requires cognitive flexibility with patience, empathy, and willingness to navigate intercultural encounters (Egitim & Sandu, 2023).

In order to reflect the multifaceted and intricate aspects of intercultural competence, Deardorff (2006) provided the "process model which outlines more of the movement and process orientation between the following components: attitudes, desired external outcome, knowledge and comprehension, skills, and desired internal outcome" (p. 256) (see Figure 1.1).

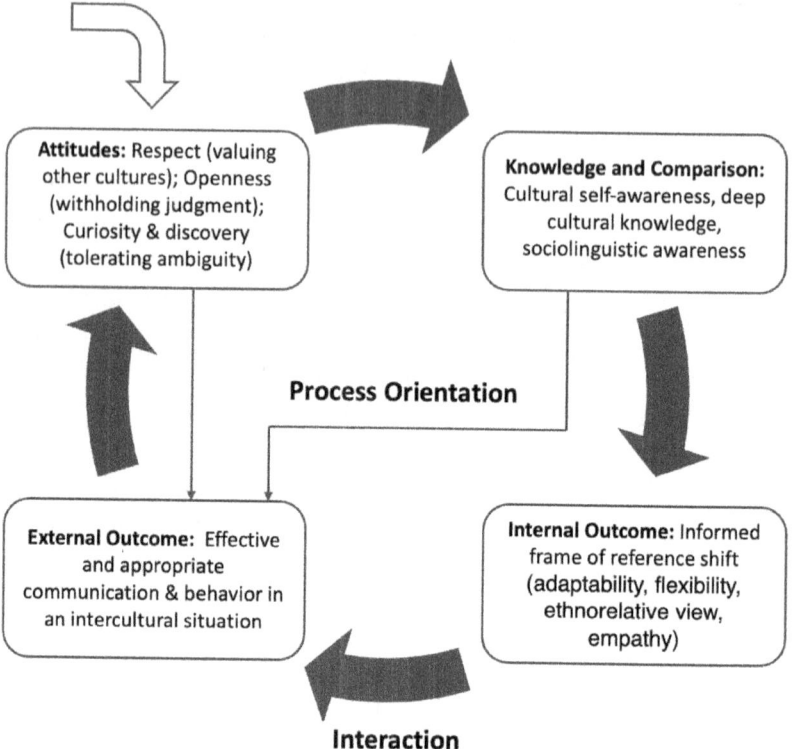

FIGURE 1.1
The Process Model of Intercultural Competence (Deardorff, 2006, p. 256)

The process model emphasizes the continuous nature of intercultural competence development, which also means that one can never reach the ultimate goal. The model's circular process is a departure from the linear models, and despite the limitations alluded to the applicability of Western-oriented models across diverse cultural contexts (Brunow & Newman, 2020), studies from non-WEIRD academic contexts used the process model to measure students' intercultural competencies (Fritz & Miyafusa, 2015; Ko et al., 2015; Richard & Doorenbos, 2016).

Similarly, Bennett's (2013) Developmental Model of Intercultural Sensitivity (DMIS) provides a framework for understanding how people experience, interpret, and interact across cultural differences. The DMIS proposes a developmental continuum, starting with more ethnocentric stages (where people are less aware of cultural differences) and progressing toward more ethnorelative stages (where individuals are better able to understand and adapt to cultural differences). Bennett (2013) emphasizes that an individual's ability to navigate intercultural interactions improves as their perceptual understanding of cultural differences becomes more complex. In other words, recognizing how cultural differences are experienced can help us predict the effectiveness of intercultural communication and tailor educational interventions to facilitate students' growth along this continuum.

While Bennett's and Deardorff's models focus on developmental processes, transformation, and progression along a continuum of intercultural sensitivity and competence, Fantini (2018) places a broader emphasis on cultural understanding and adaptability in his intercultural communicative competence (ICC) model. The ICC refers to abilities necessary for engaging with diversity during study abroad and other educational exchange experiences. It involves understanding cultural differences, adapting communication styles, and developing empathy and openness towards other cultures. Fantini (2020) emphasized the integration approach, viewing communicative competence in one's mother tongue and communicative competence in the target language as essential components of intercultural communicative competence. Conversely, "The absence of one or the other could compromise the person's ability to correctly interpret issues arising from intercultural interactions" (Egitim, 2024, p. 4). We illustrated this point earlier in the case of EWL teachers potentially misinterpreting Japanese students' needs and expectations, compared to local language teachers who prefer to use L1 as the medium of instruction due to their lack of confidence in using English. In this regard, we should start viewing language beyond a means of communication in language classrooms. Language reflects cultures, values, and beliefs that connect us with people on a deeper level, fostering empathy and understanding across cultural boundaries. Hence, treating language and culture as a "single, interrelated" process should lead to an "integrated, embodied, experiential, and transformational" learning experience for students (Shaules, 2019, p. 132).

However, intercultural competence in English language classrooms extends beyond students. Language teachers must also engage in self-reflection after intercultural encounters, assessing their own development needs regarding intercultural competence. Moreover, teachers should promote intercultural awareness through interactive activities alongside their learners' linguistic proficiency. These activities should encourage students to reflect on their own culture and recognize how their cultural background has shaped their perspectives. This is where the need for a practical, context-independent framework becomes crucial, and it serves as the central focus of this book. In the following section, we delve deeper into our *global competence* framework, designed to offer both educators and students a concrete path toward becoming globally competent individuals in English language classrooms and beyond. We will highlight the current needs of English language learners in the Asia-Pacific context, provide an overview of the ongoing reforms, and demonstrate how the framework can bridge the gap between current policies and classroom practices (see Figure 1.2).

1.4 Introduction to the *Global Competence* Framework

Despite various policy initiatives by governments to promote *global competence* through English language education in the Asia-Pacific region, the lack of practical guidelines has created a gap between policy and practice (Hofmeyr, 2023; Richter, 2022; Zhang & Bournot-Trites, 2021). In other words, the vision of globally competent citizens, as outlined in frameworks such as the Japanese government's *Global Jinzai* definition, is often overlooked in English language classrooms (Egitim, 2022a). This disconnect between what is intended and what is actually taught and assessed leads to compromises in the development of students' *global competence* in university EWL settings.

Part of the issue is that the English language is still treated as an academic subject assessed by standardized exams in the Asia-Pacific region (Zhu, 2021). Hence, the more important goal appears to be to achieve a high test score as opposed to developing skills and attitudes to thrive in global environments. This perception is further reinforced by the Test of English for International Communication (TOEIC), which is a standardized English language assessment specifically oriented toward professionals and companies in the Asia-Pacific context. The TOEIC test assesses both receptive and productive English skills, yet the latter is not generally required as receptive skills are often found sufficient by Japanese organizations who view the test as a valuable indicator of new grads' English language proficiency levels and their ability to navigate global business environments (Kamiya, 2024). Therefore, many university students feel pressured to achieve a high TOEIC score to gain an advantage in the increasingly competitive job markets.

Another issue appears to be the confusion stemming from the contrast between the policies to promote *global competence* education and the deep-rooted Confucian-Heritage education, which emphasizes standardized language education based on teacher-centered instruction (Matsuyama et al., 2019; Richter, 2022; Zhang & Bournot-Trites, 2021). In such learning environments, it would be unrealistic to promote essential components of *global competence* such as critical thinking, inquiry-based learning, creativity, and intercultural understanding.

As emphasized earlier in this book, *global competence* extends beyond language proficiency and cross-cultural knowledge. It involves understanding diverse perspectives, critically analyzing global issues, and developing a collective consciousness to address our shared challenges on a global scale. To equip students with the skills and attitudes needed to navigate these challenges in an increasingly interconnected world, a practical and context-independent framework is essential, one that this book aims to provide. Specifically, a comprehensive framework that integrates language, culture, attitudes, and values can guide education systems, institutions, and educators on how to systematically cultivate *global competence* in students. By offering clarity for curriculum design in EWL settings and beyond, such a framework can help eliminate inconsistencies. Now, let's unpack the components of the *global competence* framework we have envisioned, drawing on empirical research and our decades of experience as language educators, language learners, and immigrants who have needed to communicate and adapt across cultures.

The first component we would like to highlight is linguistic proficiency. The English language is the primary tool for expressing thoughts, feelings, and ideas as well as understanding and relating to people from different cultures in cross-cultural encounters. We divided the English language proficiency into receptive (listening and reading comprehension) and productive (speaking and writing) skills. The second component we propose is cross-cultural knowledge. This knowledge becomes more meaningful when we engage in intercultural interactions, which we view as the starting point. Through such interactions, individuals should cultivate curiosity about other cultures, regardless of whether the experience is positive or negative. As curiosity develops, individuals are likely to seek out information about the culture, a process we refer to as 'research and discovery' in our framework (see Figure 1.2). Finally, repeating these three steps should facilitate the acquisition of meaningful cross-cultural knowledge. We believe this is a cumulative process that fosters individuals' curiosity and desire to learn more about one another, thereby creating a positive and dynamic cycle that continues.

The third component of the framework is developing adaptability in our communication style. Let's illustrate what we mean by adaptability through the experiences of the first author, Soyhan:

> *One day, I was sitting on the train and observing two Japanese university students standing in front of me. This was only a few years after I arrived in Japan in 2006. The students engaged in a conversation with each other about school matters in Japanese. However, I noticed that neither of them was making any eye contact. Their hands were mostly down, meaning they hardly*

Introduction to Four-Step Framework for *Global Competence* ♦ 17

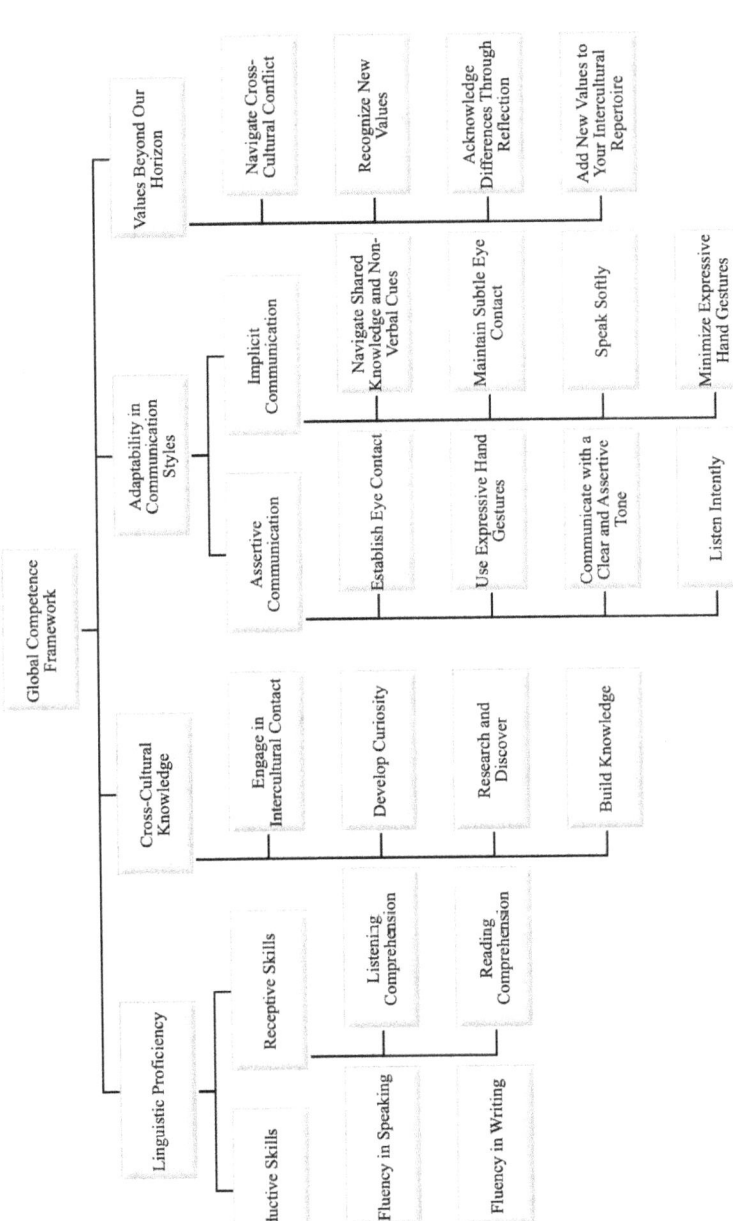

FIGURE 1.2 Global Competence Framework

> used any hand gestures. They were taking turns in the conversation. When one of them was taking the floor, the other one was nodding, yet they were both facing the train window. They were also speaking quite gently to the point that I had to make an extra effort to hear what they were saying. This implicit communication style seemed so effective in helping them get their points across without the need to raise their voice, use hand gestures, and make eye contact. I was quite astonished by how that could be possible.

In fact, this implicit and non-confrontational style of communication is the most prevalent in the Japanese context. More often than not, people can interpret each other's needs through shared knowledge, non-verbal cues, and reading between the lines. This approach helps save face and maintain harmony in social interactions. However, using the implicit communication style may compromise students' ability to effectively communicate their ideas during cross-cultural encounters even though they may have adequate English language proficiency and cultural knowledge. Avoiding eye contact with the other party may be perceived as a lack of interest in the conversation or a lack of confidence in the person's ability to communicate in Western cultural contexts. It may put the individual in an inferior position in the conversational exchange. Furthermore, speaking with a low and gentle voice and minimizing expressive hand gestures during a presentation may give the audience the impression that the presenter lacks confidence in their ability to present their ideas in a multicultural work setting.

Hence, adaptability in communication styles becomes a critical component in managing intercultural encounters effectively. We divided adaptability in communication styles into two categories: implicit communication style and assertive communication style. For Japanese students, who excel in implicit communication, developing an assertive communication style is crucial for effective intercultural communication in English. Similarly, for British students studying Japanese, learning implicit communication is essential for thriving in the Japanese context. In fact, if we think of this process as a shuttle bus route, with one end representing implicit communication and the other representing assertive communication, developing an assertive communication style should enable Japanese students to develop the cognitive flexibility to 'get off the bus' at any point along the route. The reverse applies to students from WEIRD cultures, where assertive communication is more prevalent.

In our framework, we label the first category as developing an assertive communication style when engaging in intercultural contact in English. This category consists of four steps: establishing eye contact, using expressive hand gestures, speaking in a brisk tone, and listening intently, which refers to paying close attention and demonstrating engagement with what is being said. For instance, in Japanese culture, people often nod to indicate they are listening. However, in WEIRD contexts, this gesture may be misinterpreted as agreement, sometimes causing confusion. In intercultural encounters with people from WEIRD cultures, it may be more effective to use verbal responses such as 'sure,' 'wow,' 'I see,' or 'hmm, interesting,' and to ask follow-up questions to demonstrate genuine interest in the conversation. Developing an assertive communication style requires practice, which should be facilitated by language teachers and peers. Therefore, the teacher assumes the responsibility of providing students with scaffolding and structure as a facilitator in English language classrooms.

The second category emphasizes an implicit, non-confrontational communication style. As demonstrated in the train story, this implicit style is especially useful for individuals engaged in cross-cultural communication within the Asia-Pacific context. It involves navigating shared knowledge, interpreting non-verbal cues, reading between the lines, maintaining minimal eye contact, speaking softly, and avoiding aggressive hand gestures. However, it would be overly simplistic to claim that this communication style can be generalized across the entire Asia-Pacific region. While the influence of Confucian norms, such as implicit communication, collective identity, and consensus-building, is evident in many countries within the region, the degree of non-confrontation in communication styles can vary depending on the context (Matsuyama et al., 2019; Richter, 2022; Zhang & Bournot-Trites, 2021). Therefore, the ability to adapt and navigate between assertive and implicit styles is crucial for successful cross-cultural communication, as illustrated in our shuttle bus analogy.

The final component of our *global competence* framework is adopting values beyond our horizon to thrive in global environments. As people move to new territories, they all face adaptation challenges, which are often unpredictable and hard to prepare for. To illustrate this, Soyhan will share an anecdote from a study abroad program he chaperoned in 2018:

> *When my colleagues and I chaperoned students to a university in Canada, the students faced challenges that none of us had anticipated. During that time, I made it a point to observe the students regularly to ensure that everyone was comfortable and enjoying their time in Canada. One day, while we were having lunch, one of the students shared an interesting story that highlighted the importance of recognizing values beyond our cultural horizon in developing global competence. The student recounted an experience where, while taking a shower at night, her host mother began banging on the bathroom door. The student was so shocked that she had to cut her shower short. Later, when she ran into her host mother in the living room, she was told that she had been in the shower for too long and was wasting water. After hearing her story, I explained to the students that the concept of taking a shower in Canada differs from that in Japan, where people often view it as a leisure activity to relax at night. In Japan, there is no perception of wasting water when taking a shower. However, the more fundamental point I wanted the students to grasp was the difference in values. I explained to them, "In Canada, people tend to speak their minds directly. So, if you want to communicate more easily with Canadians, you may want to embrace this value." Needless to say, it is difficult for Japanese students to fully understand this value immediately. For one thing, they are raised with the values of Honne (one's true feelings) and Tatemae (what is expected*

by society based on one's position and circumstances). Using Tatemae in Canada, however, would almost never work, as Canadians often prefer to express their true feelings directly. I shared with the students that I use Tatemae when I am with my Japanese friends and colleagues to contribute to group harmony, while I use Honne with my foreign friends, as I can express my true feelings more directly. In this way, both groups appreciate my presence. I added, 'So, from now on, when we have a problem, let's try to communicate our needs and desires more directly in Canada.' A few days later, when I checked in with the students, some of them began to complain about their lunches. They mentioned that they were tired of eating sandwiches every day. I asked, 'Am I making your sandwiches?' The students chuckled and said, 'No.' Then I asked, 'Who is making your sandwiches?' One student replied, 'My host mother.' I followed up with the final question, 'Do you remember what we need to do when we run into a problem in Canada?' The students responded, 'We need to speak our minds directly.' Some of the students decided to do just that. I taught them several polite expressions to avoid offending anyone when expressing their feelings directly. The next day, some students approached me and said that they had finally been provided with warm meals. From that point onward, those students began to express their needs and desires more directly (Egitim & Sandu, 2023, p. 168).

The essence of this anecdote is that the students did not have to abandon their own values. Instead, they embraced a new value, which helped them adapt to the new cultural environment. In this sense, unpacking our backpacks and examining our own values plays a critical role in developing cognitive flexibility (Franklin, 2014). By stretching and expanding our backpacks, we create space to include new values in our intercultural repertoire which refers to the set of skills, knowledge, attitudes, and behaviors that individuals develop to effectively navigate and engage with diverse cultural perspectives. Hence, the final component of the *global competence* framework involves navigating cross-cultural conflict, learning new values, recognizing differences, and expanding our intercultural repertoire by incorporating those new values (see Figure 1.2).

References

Bennett, J. M. (2013). *Basic concepts of intercultural communication: Paradigms, principles, and practices*. Nicholas Barley Publishing. https://lccn.loc.gov/2013005341

Bennett, J. M. (2023). Paradigmatic assumptions and developmental approach to intercultural learning. In M. Van De Berg, M. Paige, & K. H. Lou (Eds.), *Student learning abroad: What our students are learning, what they're not, and what we can do about it* (pp. 87–112). Routledge. https://doi.org/10.4324/9781003447184

Brunow, B., & Newman, B. (2020). A developmental model of intercultural competence: Scaffolding the shift from culture-specific to culture-general. In R. Criser & E. Malakaj (Eds.), *Diversity and decolonization in German Studies* (pp. 139–158). Palgrave Macmillan. https://doi.org/10.1007/978-3-030-34342-2_8

Byram, M. (1997). *Teaching and assessing intercultural communication competence*. Multilingual Matters.

Byram, M. (2009). The intercultural speaker and the pedagogy of foreign language education. In D. Deardorff (Ed.), *The SAGE handbook of intercultural competence* (pp. 321–332). Sage. https://doi.org/10.4135/9781071872987.n18

Davidson, R., & Liu, Y. (2020). Reaching the world outside cultural representation and perceptions of global citizenship in Japanese elementary school English textbooks. *Language, Culture and Curriculum*, *33*(1), 32–49. https://doi.org/10.1080/07908318.2018.1560460

Deardorff, D. K. (2006). Identification and assessment of intercultural competence as a student outcome of internationalization. *Journal of Studies in International Education*, *10*(3), 241–266. https://doi.org/10.1177/1028315306287002

Deardorff, D. (2009). *The SAGE handbook of intercultural competence*. Sage. https://doi.org/10.4135/9781071872987

Egitim, S. (2021). Collaborative leadership in English language classrooms: Engaging learners in leaderful classroom practices.

International Journal of Leadership in Education, 28(1), 1–21. https://doi.org/10.1080/13603124.2021.1990413

Egitim, S. (2022a). *Collaborative leadership through leaderful classroom practices: Everybody is a leader.* Candlin & Mynard e-publishing. https://doi.org/10.47908/22

Egitim, S. (2022b). Do Japanese students lack critical thinking? Addressing the misconception. *Power and Education*, 14(3) 1–6. https://doi.org/10.1177/17577438221107203

Egitim, S. (2022c). Voices on language teacher stereotypes: Critical cultural competence building as a pedagogical strategy. *Journal of Language, Identity & Education*, *23*(6), 925–939. https://doi.org/10.1080/15348458.2022.2070847

Egitim, S., & Sandu, R. (2023). Intercultural language education through leaderful pedagogy: A collaborative autoethnographic approach. In S. Egitim & Y. Umemiya (Eds.), *Leaderful classroom pedagogy through an interdisciplinary lens* (pp. 159–174). Springer Singapore. https://doi.org/10.1007/978-981-99-6655-4_10

Egitim, S. (2024). Does language teachers' intercultural competence influence oral participation in EFL classrooms?: Unveiling learner perspectives through a mixed methods inquiry. *Journal of Multilingual and Multicultural Development*, 1–34. https://doi.org/10.1080/01434632.2024.2306169

Engel, L. C., Rutkowski, D., & Thompson, G. (2019). Toward an international measure of global competence? A critical look at the PISA 2018 framework. *Globalization, Societies and Education, 17*(2), 117–131. https://doi.org/10.1080/14767724.2019.1642183

Estellés, M., & Fischman, G. E. (2021). Who needs global citizenship education? A review of the literature on teacher education. *Journal of Teacher Education, 72*(2), 223–236. https://doi.org/10.1177/0022487120920254

Fantini, A. E. (2018). Intercultural communicative competence in educational exchange: A multinational perspective. Routledge. https://doi.org/10.4324/9781351251747

Fantini, A. E. (2020). Reconceptualizing intercultural communicative competence: A multinational perspective. Research in Comparative and International Education, 15(1), 52–61. https://doi.org/10.1177/1745499920901948

Franklin, Y. (2014). Virtually unpacking your backpack: Educational philosophy and pedagogical praxis. *Educational Studies*, *50*(1), 65–86. https://doi.org/10.1080/00131946.2014.867219

Fritz, R., & Miyafusa, S. (2015). The ideal intercultural self-framework: A way to motivate students to develop intercultural communicative competence. *JACET International Convention Selected Papers*, *3*, 130–143. www.jacet.org/SelectedPapers/JACET54_2015_SP_3_5.pdf#page=130

Fritz, R., & Sandu, R. (2020). Foreign language and intercultural development in the Japanese context: A case study. *Language and Intercultural Communication*, *20*(6), 600–620. https://doi.org/10.1080/14708477.2020.1766480

Galloway, N., Numajiri, T., & Rees, N. (2020). The 'internationalization', or 'Englishisation', of higher education in East Asia. *Higher Education*, *80*(3), 395–414. https://doi.org/10.1007/s10734-019-00486-1

Harumi, S. (2011). Classroom silence: Voices from Japanese EFL learners. *ELT Journal*, *65*(3), 260–269. https://doi.org/10.1093/elt/ccq046

Hofmeyr, A. S. (2023). Rethinking the concept of global human resources in the Japanese higher education context. *Asia Pacific Journal of Education*, *43*(1), 62–78. https://doi.org/10.1080/02188791.2021.1889970

Holliday, A. (2006). Native-speakerism. *ELT Journal*, *60*(4), 385–387. https://doi.org/10.1093/elt/ccl030

Holliday, A. (2021). *Intercultural communication: An advanced resource book for students*. Routledge. https://doi.org/10.4324/9780367482480

Houghton, S. A. (2014). Exploring manifestations of curiosity in study abroad as part of intercultural communicative competence. *System*, *42*, 368–382. https://doi.org/10.1016/j.system.2013.12.024

Houghton, S. A., & Rivers, D. J. (2013). Introduction: Redefining native-speakerism. In S. A. Houghton & D. J. Rivers (Eds.), *Native-speakerism in Japan: Intergroup dynamics in foreign language education* (pp. 1–16). Multilingual Matters. https://doi.org/10.21832/9781847698704-004

Jon, J. E., & Yoo, S. S. (2021). Internationalization of higher education in Korea: Policy trends toward the pursuit of the SDGs. *International Journal of Comparative Education and Development*, *23*(2), 120–135. https://doi.org/10.1108/IJCED-10-2020-0073

Kamiya, N. (2024). Is the common test for University admissions in Japan enough to measure students' general English proficiency? The case of the TOEIC Bridge. *Language Testing in Asia*, *14*(1), 2. https://doi.org/10.1186/s40468-024-00272-6

Ko, B., Boswell, B., & Yoon, S. (2015). Developing intercultural competence through global link experiences in physical education. *Physical Education and Sport Pedagogy*, *20*(4), 366–380. https://doi.org/10.1080/17408989.2013.837441

Kubota, R., & Takeda, Y. (2021). Language-in-education policies in Japan versus transnational workers' voices: Two faces of neoliberal communication competence. *TESOL Quarterly*, *55*(2), 458–485. https://doi.org/10.1002/tesq.613

Lowe, R. J., & Pinner, R. (2016). Finding the connections between native-speakerism and authenticity. *Applied Linguistics Review*, *7*(1), 27–52. https://doi.org/10.1515/applirev-2016-0002

Maganaka, A. (2023). Native speakerism and employment discrimination in English language teaching. *Canadian Journal for New Scholars in Education*, *14*(1), 119–130. https://core.ac.uk/download/pdf/578306393.pdf

Mansilla, V. B., & Gardner, H. (2007). From teaching globalization to nurturing global consciousness. Learning in the global era: International perspectives on globalization and education.

DeGruyter Matsuyama, Y., Nakaya, M., Okazaki, H., Lebowitz, A. J., Leppink, J., & Van der Vleuten, C. (2019). Does changing from a teacher-centered to a learner-centered context promote self-regulated learning: A qualitative study in a Japanese undergraduate setting. *BMC Medical Education*, *19*, 152. https://doi.org/10.1186/s12909-019-1550-x

Meng, Q., Zhu, C., & Cao, C. (2018). Chinese international students' social connectedness, social and academic adaptation: The mediating role of global competence. *Higher Education*, *75*, 131–147. https://doi.org/10.1007/s10734-017-0129-x

Mikhaylov, N. S. (2016). Curiosity and its role in cross-cultural knowledge creation. *International Journal of Emotional Education*, *8*(1), 95–108. https://core.ac.uk/download/pdf/46603917.pdf

Moon, D. G. (2023). Critical reflections on culture and critical intercultural communication. In T. K. Nakayama & R. T. Halualani (Eds.),

The handbook of critical intercultural communication (pp. 57–71). Wiley. https://doi.org/10.1002/9781119745426.ch4

Noels, K. A., Yashima, T., & Zhang, R. (2020). Language, identity, and intercultural communication. In J. Jackson (Ed.), *The Routledge handbook of language and intercultural communication* (pp. 55–69). Routledge. https://doi.org/10.4324/9781003036210

OECD. (2018). *Preparing our youth for an inclusive and sustainable world: The OECD PISA global competence framework*. www.oecd.org/pisa/Handbook-PISA-2018-Global-Competence.pdf

Rathje, S. (2007). Intercultural competence: The status and future of a controversial concept. *Language and Intercultural Communication, 7*(4), 254–266. https://doi.org/10.2167/laic285.0

Reimers, F. M. (2009). Global competency. *Harvard International Review, 30*(4), 24–27. www.proquest.com/openview/79fc1e42aaa71d17d96f63f0f82a2ec7/1?pq-origsite=gscholar&cbl=32013

Richards, C. A., & Doorenbos, A. Z. (2016). Intercultural competency development of health professions students during study abroad in India. *Journal of Nursing Education and Practice, 6*(12), 89. https://doi.org/10.5430/jnep.v6n12p89

Richter, N. E. (2022). An investigation of learning English as a second language in Korea. *Journal of Problem-Based Learning, 9*(2), 77–86. https://doi.org/10.24313/jpbl.2022.00199

Sakamoto, F., & Roger, P. (2023). Global competence and foreign language education in Japan. *Journal of Studies in International Education, 27*(5), 719–740. https://doi.org/10.1177/10283153221076905

Shaules, J. (2019). *Language, culture, and the embodied mind*. Springer Nature. https://doi.org/10.1007/978-981-15-0587-4

Smith, E. C., & Luce, L. F. (1979). *Toward internationalism: Readings in cross-cultural communication*. Newbury House.

Steele, D., & Zhang, R. (2016). Enhancement of teacher training: Key to improvement of English education in Japan. *Procedia-Social and Behavioral Sciences, 217*, 16–25. https://doi.org/10.1016/j.sbspro.2016.02.007

Thomas, A., Kinast, E. U., & Schroll-Machl, S. (2010). *Handbook of intercultural communication and cooperation: Basics and areas of application*. Vandenhoeck & Ruprecht. http://library.oapen.org/handle/20.500.12657/29700

Wilkinson, J. (2020). From native speaker to intercultural speaker and beyond. In J. Jackson (Ed.), *The Routledge handbook of language and intercultural communication* (pp. 283–298). Routledge. https://doi.org/10.4324/9781003036210

Yamada, E. (2021). Investigating the roles of first language (L1) speakers in lingua franca communication in multicultural classrooms: A case study of Japanese as a lingua franca (JLF). *Journal of English as a Lingua Franca*, *10*(2), 285–311. https://doi.org/10.1515/jelf-2021-2057

Zhang, H., & Bournot-Trites, M. (2021). The long-term washback effects of the National Matriculation English Test on college English learning in China: Tertiary student perspectives. *Studies in Educational Evaluation*, *68*, 100977. https://doi.org/10.1016/j.stueduc.2021.100977

Zheng, J., & Kapoor, D. (2021). State formation and higher education policy: An analytical review of policy shifts and the internationalization of higher education in China between 1949 and 2019. *Higher Education*, *81*, 179–195. https://doi.org/10.1007/s10734-020-00517-2

Zhu, G. (2021). A prism of the educational utopia: The East Asian educational model, reference society, and reciprocal learning. *Discourse: Studies in the Cultural Politics of Education*, *42*(6), 943–957. https://doi.org/10.1080/01596306.2020.1714547

2

Intercultural Language Education: Treating Language and Culture as One

Soyhan Egitim and Seiko Harumi

2.1 The Perception of Intercultural Education in the Asia-Pacific Region

Intercultural education is a reflective, socio-educational practice focused on social and cultural transformation through equal rights, equity, and positive interaction between different cultures (Cárdenas-Rodríguez & Terrón-Caro, 2021). It aims to promote openness to diversity, tolerance, and respect for others through exposure to different cultures, traditions, customs, and histories. It starts with creating inclusive learning spaces where students feel comfortable sharing their perspectives through respectful dialogue and curiosity about other cultures (Bennett, 2013). Furthermore, intercultural education encourages students to view global and domestic issues from a critical lens and engages them in constructive disagreements through diverse cross-cultural content (Byram, 2009; Egitim, 2024; Galloway et al.,

2020). Exposure to diverse views not only helps break down stereotypes but also promotes empathy. It encourages students to see issues beyond their cultural lens and appreciate different perspectives (Fantini, 2018; Spencer-Oatey et al., 2022).

While intercultural education is premised on exploring diverse cultures, identities, and perspectives to promote tolerance and openness, the traditional Confucian values of implicit communication, collective identity, harmony, and consensus-building are still influential in the Asia-Pacific region and stand in sharp contrast to these endeavors (Egitim, 2022; Matsuyama et al., 2019; Richter, 2022; Zhang & Bournot-Trites, 2021). Despite the recent increases in the number of immigrant workers and minorities, multiculturalism is still perceived with skepticism, with the policies emphasizing assimilation rather than maintaining minority heritages and promoting equal opportunities in these societies (Iwabuchi et al., 2016; Nagy, 2014). The implication of such policies in educational settings is that assimilation-focused curricula, which prioritize conformity over the preservation of minority cultures, overlook the importance of multicultural education (Kim, 2020).

As rapid globalization continues to impact societies, the countries in the Asia-Pacific region are grappling with the complexities of multicultural education as they work towards creating inclusive and equitable learning environments. In this effort, English language education remains a key component. English is widely viewed as the lingua franca, which allows people from diverse linguistic backgrounds to communicate effectively—a vital tool in multicultural settings. Learning English can facilitate cultural exchange and understanding between students from different backgrounds through literature, media, and communication, which helps cultivate a more inclusive and empathetic worldview. Furthermore, many educational resources, including textbooks, research papers, and online courses, are available primarily in English, highlighting the importance of English language education. However, to nurture well-rounded individuals who are not only proficient in English but also culturally aware and adaptable, it has become evident that integrating intercultural content into English as a world language (EWL) classes is essential. Thus far, the Asia-Pacific region has seen significant shifts in educational policies to align with the demands of globalization. However, a gap remains between these policy goals and their implementation in practice. Despite the progressive policies, many educational institutions still struggle to integrate intercultural content effectively into EWL curricula. This gap highlights the difficulty of turning policy into reality, emphasizing the need for ongoing efforts to close this divide.

2.2 Challenges and Opportunities of Integrating Intercultural Education into English as a World Language Curriculum

With the growing impact of globalization and increased student mobility, intercultural education has become increasingly important in language classrooms. Hence, over the past few decades, various educational policies have been implemented in Japan, China, and Korea to create an educational environment aligned with globalization. In Japan, the goals and content of EWL education, a more inclusive term used instead of foreign language education, have been revised across elementary, lower secondary, and upper secondary schools to promote cross-cultural understanding through interactive language activities in English language classes. The new pre-tertiary English language education focused on encouraging students to communicate their thoughts and feelings in practical contexts and clarify what students can do using world languages during real-life intercultural encounters (Fritz & Sandu, 2020; Ngai et al., 2020).

China has also undergone significant educational reforms, including curriculum changes, teacher training, and modernization of teaching methods. Efforts were mainly focused on improving the quality of education to promote equity and inclusivity (Kitamura et al., 2022). On the other hand, Korean universities have established graduate schools of international studies, summer programs, and exchange initiatives to foster global perspectives. The country also took measures to support students facing barriers during the pandemic, including subsidizing devices for remote learning (Kang, 2022).

While policies and reforms emphasize multiculturalism and global citizenship education, practical implementation remains a challenge in the Asia-Pacific region. Especially, the absence of a practical framework to deliver intercultural education creates a disconnect between policy and practice. Classroom dynamics often diverge from the intended outcomes outlined in current policies. In this regard, intercultural education remains somewhat disconnected from EWL curricula.

In university EWL settings, promoting linguistic proficiency appears to be prioritized over intercultural competence (IC) development despite the well-documented benefits of integrating intercultural language education (Kamiya, 2024; Kang, 2022; Zhu, 2021). Because employers highly value test scores, many students prioritize achieving high scores on exams like the TOEIC over developing intercultural skills to secure employment after graduation. Many programs in Japan, Taiwan, and Korea go to great lengths to make TOEIC scores a graduation requirement (Cho, 2012; Hsieh, 2017; Takahashi, 2012). Hence, students are left with no choice but to focus all their energy on accomplishing this goal.

Furthermore, there appears to be a lack of understanding on the part of language teachers regarding how to integrate intercultural content into English language classes. In this regard, the shortage of intercultural training opportunities for language teachers acts as a major deterrent. Intercultural education involves reflective socio-educational practices aimed at promoting social and cultural transformation in educational settings. Providing intercultural education in English language classes involves teaching culturally sensitive content while dealing with individuals with diverse values and perspectives. By emphasizing equal rights, equity, and positive interactions among diverse cultures, intercultural education also ensures that students learn to recognize cultural diversity, value egalitarian relationships, and take a stance against racism and discrimination (Cárdenas-Rodríguez & Terrón-Caro, 2021). Hence, managing this process essentially requires comprehensive teacher training (LaScotte &

Peters, 2021). Knowing how to use culturally relevant materials, incorporate global perspectives, and encourage dialogue among students from various backgrounds can contribute significantly to creating inclusive, intercultural classrooms that can provide opportunities for all students to thrive.

Furthermore, developing an instructional model that explicitly incorporates intercultural learning into the EWL curriculum can be of great aid. Having a sound framework can ensure that students are given opportunities to explore cultural topics, engage in cross-cultural discussions, and reflect on their own cultural assumptions through respectful dialogue, and maintain their curiosity about other cultures. The absence of these perspectives can discourage English language teachers from incorporating intercultural learning into their syllabi. When the lack of training opportunities is coupled with the pressure to help students achieve high test scores, integrating intercultural education into English language classes becomes a lower priority for language teachers.

The prevalence of native-speakerism in the Asia-Pacific region poses another challenge to achieving multicultural education endeavors (Lowe & Pinner, 2016). The belief that native speakers possess superior language skills and cultural knowledge often leads to an unequal power dynamic, affecting the perceptions of students and institutions, and making it difficult for non-native teachers to find employment (Egitim, 2022a; Maganaka, 2023). Many language schools and businesses prefer hiring native speakers due to market demands. According to Holliday (2015), the concept of native speakerism acts as a hindrance to promoting multicultural education. It represents a pervasive cultural bias—an undervaluation of the cultural contributions made by teachers labeled as non-native speakers. This label not only characterizes their connection to English but also implies a cultural deficit rooted in non-Western stereotypes.

It perpetuates the belief that English is most valid, prestigious, and desirable when owned and controlled by those born into it as their first language. Moreover, native-speakerism could also undermine the value of native-speaker teachers, turning them into commodities sought after by an industry fixated on the idea of native speakers. The idealized English language teacher was often depicted as a Caucasian male with an entertaining persona, which hinders native-speaker teachers' ability to establish a professional identity beyond their appearance and personality (Egitim, 2022b). On the other hand, these hiring practices influenced by the Caucasian English teacher stereotypes can also disadvantage English teachers of color who cannot live up to the stereotypical expectations due to their nationality, gender, or ethnic background, despite having the necessary credentials and teaching experience (Appleby, 2014). Therefore, dismantling native speakerism and believing in the cultural contribution of all teachers, regardless of their background, is essential to fostering acceptance, tolerance, and openness in English language classrooms. One realistic approach to dismantling the unattainable native speaker ideal is to promote near-peer role models (NPRMs) in English language classes, which we have discussed thoroughly in section 3.1 (Hooper et al., 2025).

The importance of intercultural education in English language classes cannot be overstated. While linguistic proficiency remains crucial, integrating intercultural learning must be an educational priority for all language teachers, administrators, and policymakers. To address the challenges we mentioned, intercultural training opportunities for language teachers should be provided to equip them with the necessary knowledge and understanding to develop instructional models that explicitly incorporate intercultural learning in English language classrooms in the Asia-Pacific context. By doing so, we can promote IC alongside language proficiency and equip students to thrive in our increasingly diverse societies.

2.3 Pragmatic Perspectives on L2 Use

The significant interconnection between language and culture in second language (L2) learning is also reflected in the field of Pragmatics. Pragmatics concerns social language use in interactions, such as an informal chat with friends in a café or a formal context like a job interview. It also includes language use in L2 classrooms when learners encounter a new language and culture. Pragmatics examines why language users interact differently in diverse socio-cultural settings (Cohen, 2018; Kramsch, 1998; Roever, 2022; Thomas, 1983), reflecting our cultural diversity. The ability to communicate with those from different cultural backgrounds is referred to as 'pragmatic competence,' defined as 'the ability to communicate your intended message with all its nuances in any sociocultural context and to interpret the message of your interlocutor as it was intended' (cited in Cohen, 2018, p. xi). To be a competent user of L2, previous studies (Cohen, 2018; Roever, 2022) specify aspects of L2 pragmatic abilities. Cohen (2018) specifically suggests the following receptive and productive abilities: speech act performance such as requesting, apologizing, understanding non-literal meanings of expressions, politeness, and conversational management skills in social interaction. The final component of conversational skills is called 'interactional competence by Hall and Pekarek Doehler (2011). This refers to the ability to maintain conversation in sequence during collaborative talk-in-interaction. When considering the pragmatic aspects of L2 interaction, we notice that language skills and cultural knowledge are closely intertwined and indispensable for effective intercultural communication.

However, as discussed in section 1.1, recent studies (Fantini, 2018; McConachy & Liddicoat, 2022) have critically addressed the fact that the integration of two key aspects—IC and L2 pragmatic competence—has yet to be achieved in both L2 learning and intercultural education, despite being mutually indispensable aspects of social interaction. Opportunities to nurture cultural sensitivity are needed both in the language classroom and in teacher training. For example, McConachy and Liddicoat (2022) point out that within existing models of IC or interactional communicative competence, language is often omitted or regarded as a general part of communication. The invisibility of language within the concept of IC is further emphasized. The separation of intercultural from language competencies obscures the points at which the ability to understand and use language itself necessitates awareness of how culture shapes meaning (McConachy & Liddicoat, 2022, p.4).

Concrete examples in practice reveal that English language teachers often focus on abstract concepts such as adaptability and empathy, or on visible cultural practices like festivals and language use. This emphasis illustrates a marginalized view of these concepts in practice, as shown in Schauer's (2006) study. Harumi's (2023b) review of the use of silence as part of interactional competence in EWL contexts in Japan highlights a significant gap between teachers' and learners' awareness of the invisible pragmatic aspects of L2 learning and the pedagogical suggestions made in scholarly discussions. According to Harumi (2023b), this gap is also reflected in L2 teaching materials, which underscores the need to integrate intercultural and pragmatic aspects of interaction into broader educational contexts.

However, it is important to note that the pedagogical approaches to L2 pragmatics and intercultural education share a common goal. Both move away from narrow, fixed views of L2 pragmatic acquisition based on native speakers' norms, instead highlighting the dynamic ways in which L2 learners can exercise their agency and develop intercultural awareness in language learning. As McConachy and Liddicoat (2022) argue that it is crucial to consider "diverse understandings of what it means to use language appropriately in context and how language learners can be encouraged to develop a sense of ownership over their language use" (p. 3), a concept explored in the leaderful classroom practices framework proposed by Egitim (2021; 2022a; Egitim & Umemiya, 2023).

Now, we turn our attention to an important aspect of L2 pragmatic practice, IC, which is a fundamental component of collaborative social interaction, involving the ability of interactants to effectively manage a conversation. Specific competencies of IC include turn-taking practices such as initiating turns, developing topics, repairing interactions, and utilizing non-verbal interactional resources, such as the use of silence in collaborative discourse. Misunderstandings arising from differences in the use of interactional resources across communities have been widely documented since the 1980s in studies examining socio-cultural variations in language use. For instance, Tannen (1981) examined the fast-paced conversational style of Jewish New Yorkers and compared them with those of non-Jewish American English speakers. She found that differences in the pace of speech and turn-taking practices could lead to misunderstandings of a speaker's intent, ranging from perceived friendliness to perceived aggressiveness.

When it comes to L2 language learners' or international students' experiences, there are other examples in which key aspects of IC, such as turn-initiation, topic development, interactional repair, and silence have been reported in various L2 learning contexts, by learners in their home country and the target culture. Turner and Hiraga's study (2003) explored a Japanese postgraduate student's turn-taking practices during a tutorial session at a British university. They found that the student, who was majoring in Art, lacked turn-initiation and topic development during the session. In a follow-up interview, it was revealed that the tutor expected the student to initiate the discussion by asking questions about her project. However, the tutor was puzzled by the interaction, as the student mostly replied with a few words and showed no intention to elaborate on her answers or initiate questions. On the other hand, the student followed the Japanese way of interacting with a tutor, waiting for the teacher's initiation to show respect rather than self-initiating interaction. This kind of invisible cross-cultural misunderstanding has also been reported elsewhere. A Chinese postgraduate student, Qiang, reading her master's degree at an Australian university, found that her Mexican classmate misinterpreted Chinese students' classroom silence:

> *One day, when we were discussing my dissertation project on Chinese international students, I told her how my participants remained silent in class for fear of wasting others' time listening to their "unprofessional" remarks. Verónica was astonished. She used to believe that Chinese students lacked interest in studying, hence the silence. She said everyone has the right to express themselves in class, even if they are not 100% correct. I*

can still recall the puzzled look on her face when she asked me why the Chinese would think otherwise (Arasaratnam-Smith & Deardorff, 2023, p. 151).

As seen above, both Qiang and Verónica had their own ways of understanding the silence of Chinese students and how and why ideas are expressed or withheld in the classroom. It was only after sharing their thoughts that they realized Chinese students' silence was interpreted differently. Regarding the use of silence in L2 interaction, Dr. Andrew Cohen, a learner of Japanese and an expert in L2 pragmatics, offers an opposing perspective. Cohen has studied the pragmatic use of L2s, including Chinese, French, Hebrew, and Japanese. He acknowledges the positive, implicit use of classroom silence to signal non-understanding EWL contexts in Japan, drawing on studies by Galloway and Rose (2015), Harumi (2011), and Kidd (2016). As a learner of Japanese, he experienced the misuse of silence and fillers such as *eeto* (well) or *ano* (uhm) in a conversation with a native Japanese speaker during a tandem language exchange. However, he noted that he learned the invisible interactional rules through his mistakes:

> *Here is an example from just one of the languages that I have dealt with: when studying Japanese, I learned that I could fill my pauses with eeto or ano, and so I did my best to fill as many pauses as I could that way. Then, eventually, my Japanese tandem partner at the time pointed out to me with all due deference that I was overusing filled pauses. She explained to me that natives preferred to use silence or nonverbal cues* more (Cohen, 2018, p. 24).

Based on his explanation, he appeared to have adopted English interactional rules to fill silence and maintain the conversation by using fillers, as suggested by Sacks et al. (1974). This highlights that one second of silence after a question can indicate interactional problems in English discourse. However, his overuse of fillers in Japanese created a negative impression for the Japanese speaker. His positive intention was met with discomfort from the other person. Furthermore, he shared another episode where he misinterpreted a Japanese English speaker's silence as a sign of relinquishing the floor, but it was not:

> *As a chair of a session at a language assessment conference at a kibbutz in the mountains near Jerusalem, I once led a round of applause for a Japanese speaker of English when I interpreted an extended pause as meaning that the speaker had ended his remarks when he had not. So in this case, it was a matter of misinterpreting silence. So embarrassed at my faux pas, I felt like crawling under the table (Cohen, 2018, p. 197).*

Based on these anecdotes, misunderstandings frequently arise from different interpretations of specific and invisible interactional resources, such as turn initiation or the use of silence, in various socio-cultural contexts and across different languages. Similar culturally oriented misunderstandings or differing interpretations of classroom interaction are common in many second or foreign-language classrooms (House, Kasper & Ross, 2003). These misunderstandings can occur between students and teachers in monolingual settings or among students in multilingual classrooms when L2 learners come from diverse cultural backgrounds. Different interpretations can also arise between first-language (L1) English-speaking teachers and non-L1 English-speaking teachers (Cohen, 2018; Harumi, 2011). Such socio-cultural and interactional differences can inhibit learners from participating in classroom activities or affect teachers' well-being, potentially leading to psychological discomfort or burnout. For example, Japanese English language learners' silence has been understood as a source of teachers' anxiety or psychological dilemmas, impacting teachers' well-being (Schachter, 2023). Awareness of these differences is the first step for all learners and teachers involved in L2 or world language learning and teaching. In the next section, we will explore how to address these interactional and perceptual differences, tackling issues in intercultural communication while deepening our cultural sensitivity in diverse socio-cultural contexts.

2.4 Cultivating Cross-Cultural Understanding Through Intercultural Encounters

As stated in our *global competence* framework, building cross-cultural knowledge is a critical step toward developing *global competence*, a goal recognized in recent educational reforms in the Asia-Pacific region (Kamiya, 2024; Kang, 2022; Zhu, 2021). In response to the globalized educational environment, the Ministry of Education, Culture, Sports, Science and Technology in Japan has implemented significant reforms since 2011. At the elementary level, English language activities were increased to twice a week, aiming to enhance students' exposure to cross-cultural knowledge while nurturing their communication skills. At the secondary level, the focus shifted toward developing students' ability to understand abstract content and communicate fluently with English speakers in various cross-cultural settings. Through such exchanges, it was hoped that students would cultivate an interest in and curiosity about other cultures (Nakayama, 2020). Similarly, between 2015 and 2020, Korea revised its national curriculum for primary and secondary education, shifting from a knowledge-based approach to a competence-based, student-centered one with an emphasis on enhancing students' exposure to cross-cultural understanding (Kang, 2022). Furthermore, in Japan, China, and Korea, more cultural content from different parts of the world was integrated into English language coursebooks to raise students' cross-cultural knowledge while also developing their English language proficiency.

Cultural contents in English language coursebooks play an important role in raising learners' comprehension of the target language and their understanding of related cultural knowledge and values (Xiong et al., 2022). These materials are essential semiotic resources that can influence young learners' perception and holistic development. Bilingual young learners negotiate their identity between native and target language cultures, experiencing it through verbal and visual modes in learning materials. These learners navigate their sense of self by engaging with both their native and target language cultures, often encountering this process through multimodal means—combining verbal and visual modes of communication. Therefore, exposure to learning materials—such as English language coursebooks—plays a crucial role in shaping their perceptions of self and others. However, as beneficial as English language coursebooks might be, mere exposure to coursebooks to develop IC would be an overly optimistic expectation. While cross-cultural knowledge gained from these materials can fulfill a basic need, it typically does not go far enough to stimulate deeper curiosity. As a matter of fact, research has shown that cross-cultural knowledge becomes more meaningful when it is sparked by real intercultural encounters, which foster deeper curiosity (Arasaratnam-Smith & Deardorff, 2023; Byram, 2009).

Let's delve into this concept further. Intercultural communication offers a unique opportunity for mutual learning (Bennett, 2009). When individuals engage directly with others from different backgrounds, they gain insights into diverse perspectives, customs, and communication styles. This firsthand experience helps us see commonalities beyond our differences, fosters empathy, breaks down stereotypes and promotes mutual understanding. Therefore, cultural exchange plays a significant role in building trust and understanding among individuals from diverse backgrounds, despite the initial challenges it may pose.

As we illustrated earlier in Chapter 1, there are things coursebooks cannot teach us. We all have developed perceptions shaped by our own cultural values, beliefs, and assumptions. For instance, a Japanese student gets stopped by her Canadian host mother while taking a long shower—an unexpected situation due to the non-confrontational nature of the Japanese communication style. At first, the student was quite upset but then recognized the value of direct communication in intercultural encounters with people from Western, Educated, Industrialized, Rich, and Democratic (WEIRD) backgrounds. Similarly, students who expressed their preference for warm meals over sandwiches to their host mothers realized that direct communication was effective in Canada when they were served warm meals during the rest of their stay there. These cultural nuances are best learned through real intercultural encounters. Once individuals have gained these experiences, they can develop the curiosity to learn more about the particular cultural norm.

Curiosity plays a significant role in promoting cross-cultural knowledge creation and competence development (Mikhaylov, 2016). Within the context of intercultural communication, the term can be defined as the recognition, pursuit, and intense desire to explore novel, challenging, and uncertain events (Kashdan & Silvia, 2009). When learners are curious, they actively seek out information, ask questions, and engage with the material. Curious learners are more likely to explore beyond the textbook, discover nuances, and deepen their understanding. Intercultural encounters are what allow individuals to achieve the recognition, pursuit, and intense desire to explore beyond materials.

When individuals approach cultural differences with respectful curiosity, they can foster meaningful interactions and deeper connections (Bennett, 2009; Deardorff, 2006). Especially, Bennett (2009) highlights that cultivating an inquisitive mindset allows individuals to be receptive to multiple perspectives. This openness creates a pathway for connecting with people from diverse cultures, enabling them to break down barriers and challenge existing stereotypes. After learners develop their curiosity through real intercultural encounters, they can refer to course books or other materials to complement their understanding. For instance, the students, who grasped the value of speaking their minds directly within WEIRD contexts, researched this content further to gain a deeper understanding of this value and why they would need to adopt it to thrive in Canadian society.

The reverse is also true. Sometimes coursebook materials can spark curiosity and inspire exploration in learners. What would add depth and significance to this type of knowledge is the opportunities we create for intercultural encounters. If this knowledge can be complemented by real-world experiences, learners' motivation will be intrinsically driven by curiosity and a genuine interest in learning about themselves and others. Intrinsic motivation is rewarding and makes intercultural communication a voluntary learning process. Hence, we can create a healthy cycle of engaging in intercultural encounters, developing curiosity,

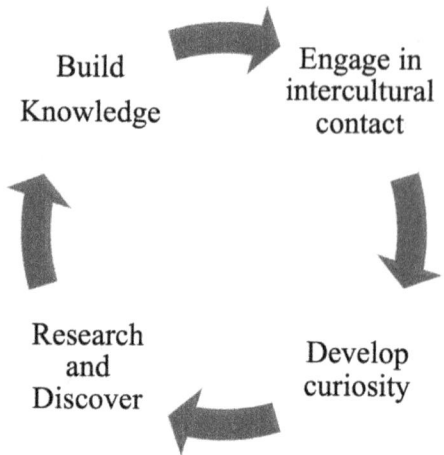

FIGURE 2.1
Cycle of Intercultural Contact, Curiosity, and Knowledge Development

Note. The cycle is a component of the *global competence* framework featured in Chapter 1.

researching, and discovering new knowledge, and adding new knowledge to our intercultural repertoire (see Figure 2.1).

2.5 Facilitating L2 Interaction in Diverse Socio-Cultural Contexts

"Language is an integral part of ourselves—it permeates our very thinking and way of viewing the world" (Kramsch, 1993, p. 77). As Kramsch addresses, the indispensable relationship between language and culture is constantly experienced in socio-culturally diverse contexts through different media, such as written texts, face-to-face interaction, online communication, and visual semiotic resources in our daily lives. As discussed in Section 1, it should be noted that L2 learners' agency in understanding the target culture, in comparison to their own, requires a cross-culturally balanced perspective. Referring to this, Kramsch (1993) states that "The ability to acquire another person's language and understand someone else's culture while retaining one's own is one aspect of the more general ability to mediate between several languages and cultures" (p. 81). Similarly, a Chinese international student, Lijianan, shares her intercultural experience as a postgraduate student in Australia:

> *I believe that acknowledging there is a cultural difference is the first step. However, interculturality does not mean giving up your own culture and language. Instead, we should try to develop and promote our own culture/language, and at the same time, always remember to respect other people's backgrounds, language, and culture. Besides, I believe interculturalism is also about exchanging ideas, interests, and knowledge with others. For example, Alison and I always like to exchange our thoughts on the same topic. It is always fascinating to find how our background knowledge, personal experiences, and culture lead us to have different values and ideas on a similar topic; There is no right or wrong answer; however, from these conversations, we can learn from each other and grow together, we also have deeper understanding of each other's culture and tend to value and respect the culture during this process* (Arasaratnam-Smith & Deardorff, 2023, p. 156).

To facilitate fruitful intercultural interaction, many studies explore effective ways to enhance such interactions, considering L2 learners' agency as a sign of ownership. It is also important to discuss other perspectives shared in empirical studies on the intercultural and pragmatic learning of East Asian languages. For the reflective process of cultivating *global competence*, we will refer to the four key components outlined in Chapter 1 (Figure 1.2): Engagement in intercultural contact, 2) Development of curiosity, 3) Research and discovery, and 4) Addition of new knowledge to the intercultural repertoire.

The first empirical study on the enhancement of interactional skills in an English as a lingua franca (ELF) context by Shigemitsu (2021) investigated the use of key conversational skills: 1) answering in extended discourse, 2) topic development, 3) listening actively and empathetically, and 4) further questioning in conversations between English language learners from Japan, Korea, and Taiwan. This study is unique in examining how participants from East Asian backgrounds interact interculturally using English. In an exercise, Japanese participants received three hours of training on these skills in English conversation before engaging in multi-party interactions. Each Japanese participant was paired with either two Korean or two Taiwanese students for conversation. While Japanese participants showed some improvements, such as using clarification questions, the overall results indicated that these learners shared similar interactional patterns. Their conversational patterns were frequently distinct from those of L1-English speakers, as they did not enhance conversations through continual questioning. Although the interactional styles among these parties differ from native-speaking norms, the study suggests that learners can choose the interactional style they prefer. This agency in interactions can help avoid unnecessary tension or uneasiness, while conventional English conversational styles can be explicitly taught.

Another ethnographic study by Lee (2021) examines how two undergraduate students from Hong Kong developed a pragmatic awareness of politeness during a short-term study abroad in the UK. The participants engaged in this project as ethnographers to explore the pragmatic use of language. They supported their findings with evidence from journal entries, interviews, and relevant documents, including social networking sites (SNS). One participant reported on the use of formulaic expressions as greetings, noting that greetings such as "How are you?" are not always practiced as taught in L2 classrooms and that a wider range of greetings exists. Despite the short duration of their time abroad, the study suggested that the students developed independent, pragmatic awareness through self-reflection and discovery. This process also helped them become more culturally sensitive to the immediate use of language and its pragmatic variations in specific contexts. In addition, intercultural experiences shared earlier by the same Chinese student, Lijianan, at an Australian university are significant as she reflects on her early years of residency. Her accounts highlight the joy of sharing certain skills or knowledge to engage in intercultural communication:

> *Allison is an Australian local student, and we met in year 10 general math class. Though we were in the same class, we barely talked to each other at first, our first formal interaction started during the second semester when she asked me for help on a specific math question. After I helped her solve the question, she praised me by saying that my way of explaining the questions is concise and clear. She said I may become a good-quality teacher in the future. I was deeply encouraged by what she said since one of my dreams is to become a teacher in the future. [...] From that point, we started to have more interactions and became good friends. [...] Her continued support really made a huge difference to me in several ways. Firstly, academically, my English abilities have been largely improved, especially my oral English, as I constantly spoke English with her. [...] In addition, we always discussed some Australian popular trends and news, these ways helped me quickly integrate into the local culture and society and allowed me to start recognizing the Australian-China cultural gaps* (Arasaratnam-Smith & Deardorff, 2023, p. 155).

Based on the findings from the studies above, it is fair to suggest that native-speaker norms are not the absolute standard for enhancing intercultural interaction, as demonstrated by the use of English among East Asian learners. Lee's (2021) study is a prime example, showing that the experience of studying abroad can provide L2 learners with opportunities to stimulate their curiosity while developing cultural awareness and reflective skills. Lijianan's account of her experiences as a postgraduate student highlights the gradual development of her cultural sensitivity, as well as the joy of sharing different values in intercultural communication. These studies suggest that language learners and international students can act as active ethnographers, critically observing the use of social language and its associated cultural values and subsequently integrating that knowledge into their own intercultural interactions.

2.6 Intercultural Language Education Through *Leaderful Classroom Practices*

As we emphasized in the previous sections, various educational reforms have been implemented to promote intercultural education in English language classes in the Asia-Pacific region in response to economic pressures and changing global trends (Egitim & Sandu, 2023). As part of this initiative, universities expanded English-medium instruction courses, providing more opportunities for students to communicate in English. The overarching goal was to enhance students' IC through active learning in world language classes (used instead of foreign language classes). While the specific content of these courses could vary, the overall focus was on developing students' ability to participate in local and global communities, understand global issues, take social and political action, compete globally, and emphasize information technology and global connectivity (Ho, 2018).

However, implementing these reforms and fostering IC is not without its challenges. Diverse classroom environments require teachers to adapt to unpredictable dynamics and varied student needs. In this context, the role of English language teachers becomes critical—they must not only deliver content but also navigate the complexities of diversity to create inclusive and engaging learning experiences. This brings us to an essential question: *What kind of leadership approach is necessary to recognize individual differences in learners and maximize their potential?* In this regard, we wish to emphasize empathy and the pivotal role it plays in transforming teachers' leadership identity. Teachers can cultivate empathy by examining their own biases, emotions, and experiences. This awareness allows them to develop an empathetic lens, enabling them to see the world through their students' perspectives. As teachers look inward and recognize their limitations, biases, and the privileged position they hold in the classroom, "They can gradually evolve as collaborative leaders who gain power from empowering others" (Egitim, 2022a, p. 26).

In 2020, Egitim (2020) developed a new pedagogical framework, *Leaderful Classroom Practices*, to raise awareness of the critical role teachers' leadership identity plays in learner development and to provide a step-by-step guide for promoting open, participatory, and democratic classroom environments. The framework is based on teachers reflecting on their leadership identity, understanding their privileged position in the classroom, and developing an empathetic lens. This perspective not only helps teachers create psychologically safe learning environments but also bridges the perceived power gap between teachers and students (Egitim, 2022a). The next phase involves engaging students in leadership responsibilities by giving them a voice in pedagogical decisions. When students recognize that their opinions matter in-class instruction and management, and when they take ownership of their learning, they gain a deeper appreciation for intercultural learning and its role in effective communication (see Figure 2.2).

As we emphasized in the previous sections, incorporating cultural elements into EWL classrooms is a challenging endeavor. Culture is multifaceted, and different people perceive it in different ways. This subjective lens makes it difficult to define and incorporate cultural aspects consistently across diverse classrooms. Furthermore, moving from the conceptualization of cultural content to its actual implementation in the curriculum poses challenges. Deciding what cultural elements to include and how to integrate them effectively requires thoughtful planning by sufficiently trained teachers. Teaching culture as simple dos and don'ts can easily lead to stereotyping rather than fostering genuine intercultural understanding among students. Liddicoat and Scarino (2013) refer to this simplistic approach to culture as mere information—a set of rules to be memorized. However, true intercultural learning goes beyond knowledge; it involves a personal transformation by adopting new cultural perspectives.

In EWL classes, when students engage in intercultural activities together, they are exposed to diverse perspectives. This

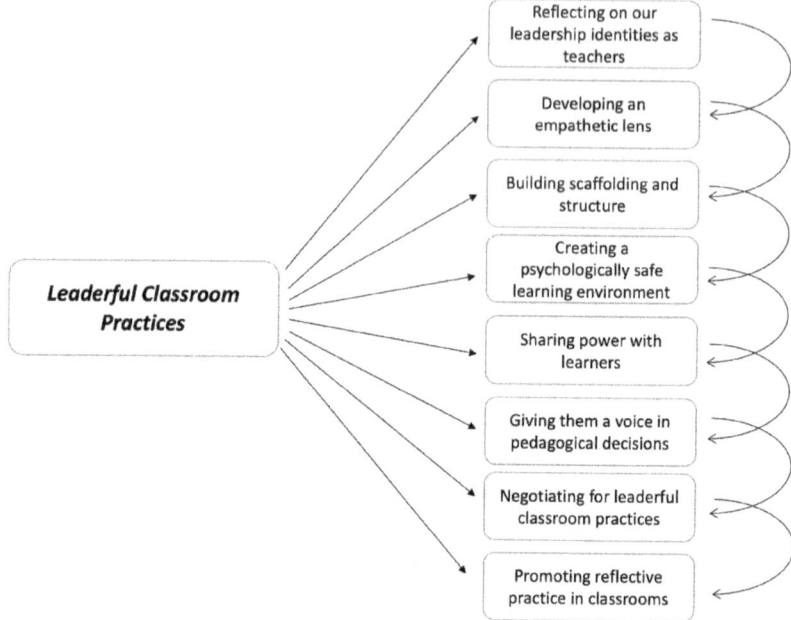

FIGURE 2.2
Leaderful Classroom Practices

Note. Figure 2.2 was adapted from the book, "Leaderful classroom pedagogy through an interdisciplinary lens: Merging theory with practice" (Egitim & Umemiya, 2023).

exposure should allow them to engage in critical reflection, which is the final step of the *leaderful classroom framework* (see Fig. 2.2). Just as teachers, through regular self-reflection, students can also develop an empathetic lens, which allows them to see issues from the viewpoints of others with different ethnic and cultural backgrounds. Active participation in reflective practice is essential for both teachers and students. "While there's no one-size-fits-all formula for developing intercultural sensitivity through English language education, creating an open, democratic, and participatory learning environment through collaborative efforts can give students opportunities to find deeper meaning in what they learn and why they learn it" (Egitim, 2022a, p. 71). As emphasized throughout this book, we are on a continuous journey here and each step along the way contributes to our IC development.

2.7 Near-Peer Role Models as Collaborative Leaders

Research has shown that leaderful group activities, workshops, and research projects facilitated by peers have a positive impact on learner engagement, motivation, and commitment (Egitim & Umemiya, 2023; Kireeti et al., 2024). Peers taking an active role in *leaderful classroom practices* could foster stronger connections among learners, contributing to a collaborative learning environment within Japanese university EWL settings (Egitim, 2022a).

In the academic literature, these peers are also described as NPRMs who can be classmates, friends, family members, teachers, or even figures we encounter through social media or other cultural channels (Murphey & Arao, 2001). A key concept underlying the idea of near-peer role modeling is to shift our focus away from vague and unattainable standards of 'native' English speakers. Instead, it highlights the importance of role models who have attained language competence through hard work and perseverance rather than mere circumstance (Hooper et al., 2025; Lingley, 2015; Murphey & Arao, 2001). NPRMs provide learners with models of language use that fall within their zone of proximal development. In essence, near-peer role modeling emphasizes hard work and perseverance, encouraging learners to aspire to their ideal selves in language learning. In other words, by creating opportunities to interact with relatable role models who have become successful in their language learning journey, peers may begin to think, "If they can do it, why can't I?" (Hooper et al., 2025, p. 2).

But how does this dynamic work in intercultural encounters? There are challenges involved in near-peer role modeling, especially when it comes to interactions between individuals from different cultural backgrounds. In the case of Japan, international students often report experiencing difficulties in engaging in meaningful intercultural interactions with their Japanese peers in university settings. Certain psychological and sociocultural factors contribute to Japanese students' hesitancy to communicate with their international peers. It goes without saying that a language barrier exists for certain students. Even if an international exchange student from Australia may be willing to engage in cross-cultural communication with Japanese students, the language barrier can at times become a significant hindrance.

Soyhan, the first author of this book, has been teaching both Japanese and international students in his *Global Competence* seminar course. In 2024, he expanded the course to include international exchange students, welcoming three Australian students into the program. His seminars are based on active learning and involve plenty of group work, discussion, and presentation activities. During the first couple of weeks, he noticed a negative dynamic between Australian and Japanese students. One Japanese student asked if she could change her group to one without any Australian students. This type of class environment was also new for Soyhan, as it involved both native-level English speakers and intermediate-level English speakers studying the same content together. Eventually, several Japanese students complained to Soyhan about struggling to understand their Australian peers, while the Australian students looked like they were also losing interest in the class due to the slower-than-usual pace of the class adjusted to Japanese students.

There are also reasons other than the language barrier. In Japan, silence holds significant value and is considered an integral aspect of communication. Conversational silence exemplifies high-context communication, where its meaning is culturally grounded (Harumi, 2011; King, 2013). Rather than indicating a lack of information, silence reflects cultural norms. It is not necessarily problematic; it aligns with the expectation of less assertiveness and the use of ambiguity as a common strategy (King & Harumi, 2020). These attributes show a communication style that is distinctly different than that of people from WEIRD societies, which also entails Australia, and it may sometimes be misinterpreted.

In a study performed by Harumi (2011), a video viewing session was held to explore how Japanese and English participants interpreted the silence of Japanese English language learners in the classroom. The study focused on specific instances where individual learners remained silent while interacting with their English teachers. Japanese informants tended to perceive silence as a face-saving 'difficulty avoidance strategy' or a form of help-seeking behavior that was acceptable or even productive if the teacher could engage the student through nonverbal cues. In contrast, many British informants viewed silence negatively, interpreting it as a sign of indifference, boredom, or laziness. Consequently, the British perspective exhibited relatively low tolerance or acceptance of silence (See the intercultural activity based on Harumi's study in Chapter 5).

Given that it would be unrealistic to expect international students to accurately interpret Japanese communication styles and adapt to them during their short-term study abroad experiences, it is not entirely surprising that Japanese students may choose to minimize their interactions with international students or avoid them altogether. Consequently, international students might experience feelings of isolation and loneliness, especially when combined with the reality of being away from their homes and families. In this regard, near-peer role modeling can be an effective strategy to promote interactions between both groups by addressing students' basic psychological needs (BPNs) satisfaction (Hooper et al., 2025). BPN is a framework proposed by Deci and Ryan (2017) that highlights three fundamental psychological needs essential for motivation, well-being, and optimal functioning:

Autonomy: The need to feel in control of one's actions and choices. Autonomy involves having the freedom to make decisions and act independently.
Competence: The need to feel effective and capable. This includes seeking opportunities to develop skills, master tasks, and achieve goals.
Relatedness: The need for social connections and positive relationships. Feeling connected to others and experiencing a sense of belonging is vital for well-being (p. 3).

Fulfilling these needs contributes to intrinsic motivation and overall satisfaction in various life domains, including education, work, and personal relationships, which is what we are trying to address here (Hooper et al., 2025). When students assume leadership roles in group and peer activities that involve students from diverse cultural backgrounds, it becomes possible to address their BPNs and, consequently, bridge the existing communication gap that hinders effective interactions.

To illustrate this, let's revisit Soyhan's classroom context, where Australian and Japanese students studied together. During the fifth week of the semester, Soyhan took all the students to a training camp at one of the university's seminar houses. He intentionally went there on his own and asked the students to meet each other downtown and go there together as a group. During their journey, Japanese students assumed leadership roles and guided international exchange students to the seminar house, which was in a secluded, remote area of Chiba, Japan. Once everyone arrived safely, they all gave presentations on their research. Australian students took the initiative during the presentations, asking questions and providing feedback to Japanese and other international students. In the evening, some Japanese students assumed leadership roles again, helping international students order dinner and guiding them to the nearest stores. The dynamic gradually shifted toward individuals taking leadership roles, when necessary, which addressed their need to feel in control, their need to feel effective and capable, and their need for social connections and positive relationships.

From that day onward, the group's bonds continued to strengthen which was positively reflected in classroom activities. Since NPRMs can exemplify good language use, communication skills, test strategies, and effective learning habits, Japanese students began to view international students as reliable role models in presentation and discussion activities. Simultaneously, international students were willing to follow the Japanese students' lead in dealing with lifestyle-related and administrative challenges. The critical point here is that individuals from both groups became role models in various situations in a multicultural classroom setting, where their relatability and shared experiences made them powerful facilitators of communication. As a result, these leaderful practices helped bridge cultural gaps, inspire learners, and promote intercultural understanding.

2.8 Leaderful Intercultural Classroom Activities in English Language Classes

In order to facilitate L2 interaction in diverse socio-cultural contexts, there is significant potential to develop and adopt facilitative pedagogical approaches for students studying L2 primarily in their home countries, guided by the *leaderful classroom framework* (Egitim, 2020). As we discussed earlier, language learning materials and resources aimed at promoting IC can create opportunities for fostering intercultural awareness and practical language use in social contexts (Jones, 2021). For instance, in EWL settings in Japan, locally produced handbooks address pragmatics-related topics such as speech acts and conversational skills. One example is a pragmatics resource series created by the Pragmatics Special Interest Group (SIG) of the Japan Association of Language Teachers (Talandis et al., 2020). The SIG has produced five different volumes of teaching resources since 2012, focusing on pragmatic aspects of L2 use to support Japan-based language teachers who are helping L2 students learning natural talk in English. Classroom resources include numerous step-by-step activities, covering themes such as speech acts, natural talk and conversational skills. These resources can also raise L2 teachers' awareness of key L2 social interactions, focused on aspects that warrant incorporation into daily classroom teaching.

Furthermore, Roever (2022) emphasizes the need for a more systematic inclusion of intercultural activities designed to enhance cultural sensitivity and awareness among L2 learners. Additionally, the development of comprehensive guidance and frameworks for teachers is essential. One promising pedagogical approach involves activities that draw learners' attention to the nuances of L2 social interaction, helping them better navigate intercultural communication. For example, Roever's study (2022) suggested the use of familiar language tasks focusing on pragmatic aspects of interaction. This includes multiple-choice or discourse completion tasks for learning speech acts, along with role plays or conversation-elicited tasks to make learners aware of features used in social interaction.

While these task types may be familiar to language teachers, their content warrants further consideration to incorporate intercultural and pragmatic aspects into L2 learning, as highlighted in the study. The pedagogical implications of these activities are thoroughly documented and discussed within the context of curriculum development, aligning with the criteria and testing frameworks of the Common European Framework of Reference (CEFR). For instance, McConachy's study (2013) utilized conversational transcripts as mediating tools in teaching materials for Japanese English language learners. The study encouraged learners to critically analyze the speech act of apologies from three perspectives: 1) meta-pragmatic focus, 2) discoursal focus, and 3) intercultural focus. These perspectives were integrated into the tasks to help learners develop emotional awareness, understand speakers' intentions, and enhance their awareness of the discoursal use of language. Moreover, the tasks fostered a reflective approach to examining how apologies are used in the learners' native languages. Similarly, Wang and Rendle-Short (2013) highlighted the effectiveness of a conversation-analytical approach in intercultural teaching and learning for Chinese Mandarin classes. Their study explored the use of *Ni hao ma* ('how are you?' in Mandarin) in telephone conversation openings, offering learners opportunities to observe and reflect on how this formulaic expression is used in interaction with a teacher compared to the textbook model dialogue.

Harumi's (2023a) study on the use of silence and repair by Japanese learners of English language draws on the framework proposed by Bao (2013) to develop speaking skills. The framework includes:

1. Conducting a needs analysis to determine the types of interactional resources to teach.
2. Using matching activities commonly employed as interactional resources for repair (e.g., the use of fillers, questioning techniques, and paying attention to keywords through repetition).
3. Analyzing transcripts from EWL and English as a second language classes to identify similarities and differences.

4. Setting up a combination of topic-based and free-talk sessions with L1 English speakers or advanced learners. These sessions aim to facilitate natural interactions during first encounters and provide opportunities for learners to reflect on their use of silence and repair.

The findings suggest that learners developed self-confidence through a series of reflective activities, raised their awareness of repair strategies, and independently set new goals for improvement. Their use of repair techniques further improved through participation in the two separate sessions. As highlighted above, there are three key elements in enhancing awareness of interactional resources in intercultural communication:

1. Explicit teaching.
2. Awareness-raising activities.
3. Opportunities for cross-cultural, natural interactions in L2 with individuals who have different interactional styles.

In relation to this, Harumi's review study (2023b) emphasizes that these three elements are essential for facilitating the pragmatic use of L2 materials through a conversation-analytic approach in intercultural communication. The study identifies four key areas where learning materials significantly contribute:

1. **Characteristics of tasks**: Tasks that are heuristic or self-discovery oriented.
2. **Mediative tools**: Resources such as transcripts, audio/visual aids, and automated transcription apps.
3. **Teachers' beliefs**: Awareness of the contrast between learners' product-oriented interactional styles and teachers' process-oriented approaches.
4. **Learners' beliefs**: Recognition of the effectiveness of materials, including heightened awareness of the functions of silence and repair, and the confidence-building benefits they offer (p. 157).

These examples focus on specific aspects of social language use, particularly IC in cross-cultural interactions. They underscore the importance of fostering reflection, scaffolding learning experiences, creating psychologically safe and engaging environments, and using learning materials to negotiate interaction. Moreover, they highlight the role of personal performance in developing intercultural sensitivity and awareness, as illustrated in Figure 2.2.

2.9 Conclusion

In Chapter 2, we explored the use of L2 in intercultural communication from two perspectives: intercultural and pragmatic. While each discipline offers a unique lens for examining the nature of L2 social interaction across cultures, empirical studies and learners' intercultural experiences clearly demonstrate that intercultural and pragmatic competencies are closely intertwined and mutually indispensable. Both learners and teachers require opportunities to nurture these competencies through pedagogical activities, such as pre-service and in-service teacher training, and engagement with learning materials that include natural interactions, either face-to-face or online (e.g., tele-tandem learning or study abroad experiences).

The integration of intercultural education in English language classrooms is not just a supplementary aspect of language learning but a critical component for fostering learners' holistic development. As highlighted in the previous sections, IC and pragmatic competence are deeply interconnected, and both need to be nurtured through intentional pedagogical activities. By providing teachers with the necessary intercultural training, and by creating opportunities for learners to engage with real-world cultural experiences, we can build a more dynamic and inclusive learning environment. Such experiences could allow learners to develop both the linguistic and social skills necessary to navigate increasingly multicultural and globalized societies. Misunderstandings in intercultural communication often arise from invisible interactional resources, such as silence or turn-taking, which vary significantly across cultures. These challenges highlight the importance of awareness and the development of empathy in both teachers and learners. As educators, fostering curiosity, openness, and a reflective mindset in learners helps them gain deeper insights into both their own and others' cultural values. The reciprocal relationship between intercultural curiosity and classroom learning materials creates a positive cycle where learners are motivated to explore, research, and build on their experiences, ultimately enhancing their IC.

Furthermore, native-speaker norms should not be viewed as the ultimate standard in intercultural interaction, as learners bring valuable cultural perspectives to the table. Language learners and international students, as active ethnographers, critically engage with cultural norms and integrate these insights into their own interactions. Yet, teaching culture in a way that avoids stereotyping requires an introspective lens, an understanding of cultural nuances, and a commitment to fostering critical thinking in students. Intercultural learning should go beyond knowledge transmission and encourage personal transformation, fostering critical reflection that challenges assumptions and builds empathy. An important aspect of this intercultural development is near-peer role modeling, where students from similar backgrounds act as role models for their peers, bridging cultural gaps and demonstrating effective communication strategies. Such role models offer authentic, relatable examples of how to navigate intercultural interactions and can serve as powerful facilitators of learning. Near-peer role models help demystify cultural practices and norms, making intercultural communication more accessible and less intimidating for learners. Building on the key steps outlined in Figure 2.2, *Leaderful Classroom Practices* (Egitim, 2020; 2021; 2022a), we will further explore how a series of reflective practices—including the development of an empathetic lens, leadership sharing, confidence building, and reflective ambition— can open new horizons for everyone involved in intercultural interactions, as we delve into the subsequent chapters.

References

Appleby, R. (2014). *Men and masculinities in global English language teaching*. Springer Nature. https://doi.org/10.1057/9781137331809

Arasaratnam-Smith, L., & Deardorff, D. (2023). *Developing intercultural competence in higher education: International students' stories and self-reflection*. Routledge. https://doi.org/10.4324/9781003229551

Bao, D. (2013). Developing materials for speaking skills. In B. Tomlinson (Ed.), *Developing materials for language teaching* (2nd ed., pp. 407–428). Bloomsbury.

Bennett, J. M. (2013). Basic concepts of intercultural communication: Paradigms, principles, and practices. *Nicholas Barley Publishing*. https://lccn.loc.gov/2013005341

Bennett, M. J. (2009). Defining, measuring, and facilitating intercultural learning: a conceptual introduction to the Intercultural Education double supplement. *Intercultural education*, 20(1), 1–13. https://doi.org/10.1080/14675980903370763

Byram, M. (2009). The intercultural speaker and the pedagogy of foreign language education. In D. Deardorff (Ed.), *The SAGE handbook of intercultural competence* (pp. 321–332). Sage. https://doi.org/10.4135/9781071872987.n18

Cárdenas-Rodríguez, R., & Terrón-Caro, T. (2021). Inclusive intercultural education in multicultural societies. *Oxford Research Encyclopedia of Education*. OUP. https://doi.org/10.1093/acrefore/9780190264093.013.2251

Cho, D. W. (2012). A level- and proficiency-based English language program of a science university in Korea. *English Teaching*, 67(4), 1–24. http://journal.kate.or.kr/wp-content/uploads/2015/01/kate_67_4_2.pdf

Cohen, A. (2018). *Learning pragmatics from native and non-native language teachers*. Multilingual Matters. https://doi.org/10.21832/9781783099931

Deardorff, D. K. (2006). Identification and assessment of intercultural competence as a student outcome of internationalization. *Journal of Studies in International Education*, 10(3), 241–266. https://doi.org/10.1177/1028315306287002

Egitim, S. (2020). *Understanding Japanese university English teachers' experiences as collaborative leaders: Engaging learners in teaching and classroom management* (Doctoral dissertation, Northeastern University). ProQuest Dissertations and Theses Global. https://doi.org/10.17760/D20394199

Egitim, S. (2021). Collaborative leadership in English language classrooms: Engaging learners in leaderful classroom practices. *International Journal of Leadership in Education*, 28(5), 1–21. http://dx.doi.org/10.1080/13603124.2021.1990413

Egitim, S. (2022a). *Collaborative leadership through leaderful classroom practices: Everybody is a leader*. Candlin & Mynard e-publishing. https://doi.org/10.47908/22

Egitim, S. (2022b). Do Japanese students lack critical thinking? Addressing the misconception. *Power and Education*, 14(3), 1–6. https://doi.org/10.1177/17577438221107203

Egitim, S. (2022). Challenges of adapting to organizational culture: Internationalization through inclusive leadership and mutuality. *Social Sciences & Humanities Open*, 5(1), 1–8. Elsevier. https://doi.org/10.1016/j.ssaho.2021.100242

Egitim, S., & Sandu, R. (2023). Intercultural language education through leaderful pedagogy: A collaborative autoethnographic approach. In S. Egitim & Y. Umemiya (Eds.), *Leaderful classroom pedagogy through an interdisciplinary lens* (pp. 159–174). Springer Nature. https://doi.org/10.1007/978-981-99-6655-4_10

Egitim, S., & Umemiya, Y. (2023). *Leaderful classroom pedagogy through a multidisciplinary lens: Merging theory with practice*. Springer Nature. https://doi.org/10.1007/978-981-99-6655-4

Egitim, S. (2024). Does language teachers' intercultural competence influence oral participation in EFL classrooms? Unveiling learner perspectives through a mixed methods inquiry. *Journal of Multilingual and Multicultural Development*, 1–34. https://doi.org/10.1080/01434632.2024.2306169

Fantini, A. E. (2018). *Intercultural communicative competence in educational exchange: A multinational perspective*. Routledge. https://doi.org/10.4324/9781351251747

Fritz, R., & Sandu, R. (2020). Foreign language and intercultural development in the Japanese context—A case study. *Language and Intercultural Communication*, 20(6), 600–620. https://doi.org/10.1080/14708477.2020.1766480

Galloway, N., Numajiri, T., & Rees, N. (2020). The 'internationalization', or 'Englishisation', of higher education in East Asia. *Higher Education*, *80*(3), 395–414. https://doi.org/10.1057/978-1-137-59733-5_6

Galloway, N., & Rose, H. (2015). *Introducing global englishes*. Routledge. https://doi.org/10.4324/9781315734347

Hall, J. K., & Pekarek Doehler, S. (2011). Emergent grammar for all practical purposes: The on-line formatting of directives in French. In J. K. Hall, J. Hellermann, & S. P. Doehler (Eds.), *L2 interactional competence and development* (Vol. 56, pp. 45–75). Multilingual Matters. https://doi.org/10.21832/9781847694072-003

Harumi, S. (2011). Classroom silence: Voices from Japanese EFL learners. *ELT Journal*, *65*(3), 260–269. https://doi.org/10.1093/elt/ccq046

Harumi, S. (2023a). Classroom silence and learner-initiated repair: Using conversation analysis-informed material design to develop interactional repertoires. *TESOL Journal*, *14*(1), e704. https://doi.org/10.1002/tesj.704

Harumi, S. (2023b). The mediative role of learning materials: Raising L2 learners' awareness of silence and conversational repair during L2 interaction. *Journal of Silence Studies in Education*, *2*(2), 145–162. https://doi.org/10.31763/jsse.v2i2.79

Holliday, A. (2015). Native-speakerism: Taking the concept forward and achieving cultural belief. In A. Swan, P. Aboshiha, & A. Holliday (Eds.), *Countering Native-Speakerism: Global perspectives* (pp. 11–25). Palgrave Macmillan. https://doi.org/10.1057/9781137463500_2

Ho, L. C. (2018). Conceptions of global citizenship education in East and Southeast Asia. In I. Davies, L. Ho, D. Kirwan, C. L. Peck, A. Peterson, E. Sant, & Y. Waghid (Eds.), *The Palgrave handbook of global citizenship and education* (pp. 83–95). Springer Nature. https://doi.org/10.1057/978-1-137-59733-5_6

Hooper, D., Egitim, S., & Hofhuis, J. (2025). Exploring the impact of near-peer role modeling on learners' basic psychological needs: Insights from English classes in Japanese Higher Education. *International Journal of Educational Research Open*, *8*(1), 1–12. https://doi.org/10.1016/j.ijedro.2024.100429

House, J., Kasper, G., & Ross, S. (2003). *Misunderstanding in social life*. Routledge. https://doi.org/10.4324/9781315838663

Hsieh, C. N. (2017). The case of Taiwan: Perceptions of college students about the use of the TOEIC® tests as a condition of graduation. *ETS Research Report Series*, *1*, 1–12. https://doi.org/10.1002/ets2.12179

Iwabuchi, K., Kim, H. M., & Hsia, H. C. (2016). *Multiculturalism in East Asia: A transnational exploration of Japan, South Korea, and Taiwan*. Rowman & Littlefield.

Jones, C. (2021). *Conversation strategies and communicative competence*. Candlin & Mynard e-publishing. https://doi.org/10.47908/19

Kamiya, N. (2024). Is the Common Test for University Admissions in Japan enough to measure students' general English proficiency? The case of the TOEIC Bridge. *Language Testing in Asia*, *14*(1), 2. https://doi.org/10.1186/s40468-024-00272-6

Kang, N. H. (2022). Multicultural education policies and practices in South Korea: A case of North Korean migrant students and science education. In M. M. Atwater (Ed.), *International handbook of research on multicultural science education* (pp. 1563–1590). Springer Nature. https://doi.org/10.1007/978-3-030-83122-6_9

Kashdan, T. B., & Silvia, P. J. (2009). Curiosity and interest: The benefits of thriving on novelty and challenge. *Social and Personality Psychology Compass*, *3*(5). https://doi.org/10.1111/j.1751-9004.2009.00210.x

Kidd, J. A. (2016). *Face and enactment of identities in the L2 classroom*. Multilingual Matters.

Kim, B. L. (2020). Multicultural education in Asia and the role of language teaching: Focusing on South Korea. *Journal of Pan-Pacific Association of Applied Linguistics*, *24*(1), 67–83. https://doi.org/10.25256/PAAL.24.1.4

King, J. (2013). *Silence in the second language classroom*. Palgrave Macmillan. https://doi.org/10.1057/9781137301482

King, J., & Harumi, S. (Eds.). (2020). *East Asian perspectives on silence in English language education* (Vol. 6). Multilingual Matters.

Kireeti, K., Egitim, S., & Thomson, B. J. (2024). Utilizing peer evaluation as a collaborative learning tool: fostering autonomy satisfaction in English presentation classes. *Language Learning in Higher Education*, *14*(2), 379–400. https://doi.org/10.1515/cercles-2024-0037

Kitamura, Y., Liu, J., & Hong, M. S. (2022). Education in East Asia: Changing school education in China, Japan, and Korea. In A. Wiseman (Ed.), *World education patterns in the global north: The ebb of global forces* and the flow of contextual imperatives (pp. 149–168). Emerald. https://doi.org/10.1108/S1479-36792022000043A010

Kramsch, C. (1993). *Context and culture in language teaching*. Oxford university press.

Kramsch, C. (1998). *Language and culture*. Oxford University Press.

LaScotte, D. K., & Peters, B. D. (2021). Fostering intercultural learning experiences in the ESL/EFL classroom. In D. L. Banegas, G. Beacon, & M. P. Berbain (Eds.), *International perspectives on diversity in ELT* (pp. 55–71). Springer Nature. https://doi.org/10.1007/978-3-030-74981-1_4

Lee, C. (2021). The process of constructing intercultural pragmatic knowledge in short-term language and culture immersion programs: Two case studies. In C. Lee (Ed.), *Second language pragmatics and English language education in East Asia* (pp. 143–163). Routledge. https://doi.org/10.4324/9781003008903

Liddicoat, A. J., & Scarino, A. (2013). *Intercultural language teaching and learning*. Wiley. https://doi.org/10.1002/9781118482070

Lingley, D. (2015). An NPRM approach to study abroad-related motivation and anxiety. In P. Clements, A. Krause, & H. Brown (Eds.), *JALT2014 conference proceedings* (pp. 299–306). JALT. https://jalt-publications.org/sites/default/files/pdf-article/jalt2014proc_030.pdf

Lowe, R. J., & Pinner, R. (2016). Finding the connections between native-speakerism and authenticity. *Applied Linguistics Review, 7*(1), 27–52. https://doi.org/10.1515/applirev-2016-0002

Maganaka, A. (2023). Native speakerism and employment discrimination in English language teaching. *Canadian Journal for New Scholars in Education*, *14*(1), 119–130. https://journalhosting.ucalgary.ca/index.php/cjnse/article/view/76500

Matsuyama, Y., Nakaya, M., Okazaki, H., Lebowitz, A. J., Leppink, J., & Van der Vleuten, C. (2019). Does changing from a teacher-centered to a learner-centered context promote self-regulated learning: A qualitative study in a Japanese undergraduate setting. *BMC Medical Education, 19*, 152. https://doi.org/10.1186/s12909-019-1550-x

McConachy, T. (2013). A place for pragmatics in intercultural teaching and learning. In F. Dervin & A. Liddicoat (Eds.), *Linguistics for intercultural education* (pp. 71–86). John Benjamins. https://doi.org/10.1075/lllt.33.05mcc

McConachy, T., & Liddicoat, A. (2022). *Teaching and learning second language pragmatics for intercultural understanding.* Routledge. https://doi.org/10.4324/9781003094128

Mikhaylov, N. S. (2016). Curiosity and its role in cross-cultural knowledge creation. *International Journal of Emotional Education, 8*(1), 95–108. https://files.eric.ed.gov/fulltext/EJ1098795.pdf

Murphey, T., & Arao, H. (2001). Reported belief changes through near-peer role modelling. *TESL-EJ, 5*(3), 1–15. www.tesl-ej.org/wordpress/issues/volume5/ej19/ej19a1/

Nagy, S. R. (2014). Politics of multiculturalism in East Asia: Reinterpreting multiculturalism. *Ethnicities, 14*(1), 160–176. https://doi.org/10.1177/1468796813498078

Nakayama, A. (2020). Three educational approaches responding to globalization in Japan. Global Citizenship Education: *Critical and International Perspectives,* 45–55. https://doi.org/10.1007/978-3-030-44617-8_4

Ngai, P. B., Yoshimura, S. M., & Doi, F. (2020). Intercultural competence development via online social networking: The Japanese students' experience with internationalization in US higher education. *Intercultural Education, 31*(2), 228–243. https://doi.org/10.1080/14675986.2019.1702289

Richter, N. E. (2022). An investigation of learning English as a second language in Korea. *Journal of Problem-Based Learning, 9*(2), 77–86. https://doi.org/10.24313/jpbl.2022.00199

Roever, C. (2022). *Teaching and testing second language pragmatics and interaction: A practical guide.* Routledge. https://doi.org/10.4324/9780429260766

Ryan, R. M., & Deci, E. L. (2017). *Self-determination theory: Basic psychological needs in motivation, development, and wellness.* The Guilford Press. https://doi.org/10.1521/978.14625/28806

Sacks, H., Schegloff, E. A., & Jefferson, G. (1974). A simplest systematics for the organization of turn-taking for conversation. *Language, 50*(4), 696–735. https://doi.org/10.1016/B978-0-12-623550-0.50008-2

Schachter, J. (2023). Tracking foreign language teachers' emotional reactions to students' silence: An autoethnographic case study. *Journal of Silence Studies in Education, 2*(2), 82–101. https://doi.org/10.31763/jsse.v2i2.68

Schauer, G. (2006). Pragmatic awareness in an EFL and ESL context: Contrast and development. *Language Learning, 56*(2), 269–318. https://doi.org/10.1111/j.0023-8333.2006.00348.x

Shigemitsu, Y. (2021). Being an active listener in unacquainted English conversations in Korean, Chinese, and Japanese intercultural settings: A case study for thinking about teaching speaking skills. In C. Lee (Ed.), *Second language pragmatics and English language education in East Asia* (pp. 95–116). Routledge. https://doi.org/10.4324/9781003008903

Spencer-Oatey, H., Franklin, P., & Lazidou, D. (2022). *Global fitness for global people: How to manage and leverage cultural diversity at work.* Castledown Publishing. https://doi.org/10.29140/9780648184430

Takahashi, J. (2012). An overview of the issues on incorporating the TOEIC test into the university English curricula in Japan. *Journal of English Language and Literature, 4*, 127–138. https://cir.nii.ac.jp/crid/1050282812955488640

Talandis, J., Ronald, J., Fujimoto, D., & Ishihara, N. (eds). (2020). *Pragmatics undercover: The search for natural talk n EFL textbooks.* JALT Pragmatics SIG, JALT Publications.

Tannen, D. (1981). New York Jewish conversational style. *International Journal of the Sociology of Language, 30*, 133–149.

Thomas, J. (1983). Cross-cultural pragmatic failure. *Applied Linguistics, 4*(2), 91–112. https://doi.org/10.1093/applin/4.2.91

Turer, J., & Hiraga, M. (2003). Misunderstanding teaching and learning. In J. House, G. Kasper, & S. Ross (Eds.), *Misunderstanding in social life* (pp. 154–172). Routledge. https://doi.org/10.4324/9781315838663

Wang, Y., & Rendle-Short, J. (2013). Making the 'invisible' visible: A conversation analytic approach to intercultural teaching and learning in the Chinese Mandarin language classroom. In F. Dervin & A. Liddicoat (Eds.), *Linguistics for intercultural education* (pp. 113–136). John Benjamins. https://doi.org/10.1075/lllt.33.07wan

Xiong, T., Feng, D., & Hu, G. (2022). Researching cultural knowledge and values in English language teaching textbooks: Representation, multimodality, and stakeholders. In T. Xiong, D. Feng, & G. Hu (Eds.), *Cultural knowledge and values in English language teaching materials: (Multimodal) representations and stakeholders* (pp. 1–18). Springer Nature. https://doi.org/10.1007/978-981-19-1935-0_1

Zhang, H., & Bournot-Trites, M. (2021). The long-term washback effects of the National Matriculation English Test on college English learning in China: Tertiary student perspectives. *Studies in Educational Evaluation*, *68*, 100977. https://doi.org/10.1016/j.stueduc.2021.100977

Zhu, G. (2021). A prism of the educational utopia: The East Asian educational model, reference society, and reciprocal learning. *Discourse: Studies in the Cultural Politics of Education*, *42*(6), 943–957. https://doi.org/10.1080/01596306.2020.1714547

3

Adaptability in Communication Styles Balancing Assertiveness and Subtlety

Soyhan Egitim and Seiko Harumi

3.1 Balancing Assertiveness and Subtlety in Intercultural Exchanges

Effectively navigating the complexities of global interactions requires a deep understanding of the dynamics of communication across cultures (Bowe et al., 2014). While high language proficiency and cross-cultural knowledge provide a solid foundation for gaining *global competence*, they are not sufficient on their own to ensure successful intercultural communication. In our increasingly interconnected world, the ability to adapt to diverse communication styles is essential for meaningful interactions across cultural boundaries (Gudykunst et al., 1996; Jonasson & Lauring, 2012). Some cultures value direct communication, while others may favor a more implicit style. Gestures, eye contact, and personal space can also vary greatly between cultures. In order to express ourselves effectively in cross-cultural encounters, we may need to develop intercultural flexibility to adapt to those different circumstances. This flexibility allows individuals to bridge cultural gaps and foster mutual understanding.

However, people tend to assume that their way of communicating is universally understood and accepted, and therefore, others will naturally adapt to them in cross-cultural interactions (Jerath, 2021; Wierzbicka, 2010; Wilczewski & Alon, 2023). Some individuals may view their own culture as the 'norm' and neglect to see the ways people from different cultural backgrounds interact, while others may not be aware of the nuances and differences in communication styles across cultures (Wilczewski & Alon, 2023). Furthermore, individuals may experience greater comfort when communicating in a familiar manner, which may, in turn, lead them to anticipate that others will adapt to their preferred communication style.

The third step of our framework emphasizes developing flexibility rather than imposing a certain style of communication to allow for more adaptability and responsiveness to different cultural settings (see Chapter 1, Figure 1.1). Let us elaborate on this point further. We categorized communication styles into two distinct types: the assertive communication style, commonly observed in WEIRD contexts, and the implicit communication style, often seen in Asian societies influenced by Confucian norms. The assertive communication style emphasizes directness, clarity, and self-expression. People are encouraged to express their thoughts, feelings, and needs openly and honestly, even if it means disagreeing or confronting others (Egitim & Umemiya, 2023; Pipas & Jaradat, 2010; Singhal & Nagao, 1993). On the other hand, implicit communication tends to be more indirect and context-dependent. In these societies, harmony, respect, and maintaining relationships are prioritized over self-expression. Hence, people may rely on non-verbal cues, context, and shared understanding to convey their messages in a subtle way (Egitim, 2022; Wilson & Kolaiti, 2017). Our *global competence* framework does not intend to recommend one approach over another. Instead, we emphasize developing students' flexibility through training and awareness of these distinct styles, so that we can adapt to different environments when we interact cross-culturally. To illustrate this process, let's use the shuttle bus route analogy, with one end of the route representing implicit communication and the other end representing assertive communication. Developing an assertive communication style would allow students, who are accustomed to implicit communication, to gain the cognitive flexibility to 'get off the bus' at any point along the way. The reverse applies to students from WEIRD cultures, where assertive communication is more prevalent. With this cognitive flexibility, students can adjust their communication style, becoming more implicit or assertive depending on the person they are interacting with.

3.2 Exploring Communication Styles Across Cultures: Why Do We Communicate the Way We Do?

The influence of the cultural environment we grow up in on our communication styles cannot be understated. Different cultures have different norms, values, and expectations around communication, which can affect everything from our body language to the way we structure our sentences. Take, for example, in some cultures, maintaining eye contact is seen as a sign of confidence and attentiveness, while in others, it might be considered rude or confrontational. Similarly, gestures, facial expressions, and other non-verbal cues can have different meanings across cultures. In Japan, avoiding direct eye contact is often viewed as a sign of respect and politeness (Uono & Hietanen, 2015). People also believe that it can also be a way to show modesty and avoid confrontation. In China and Korea, indirect eye contact is viewed as a sign of politeness and respect, especially when interacting with someone older or more senior. This practice is rooted in Confucian ideals, which emphasize hierarchy and respect. Contrarily, if you avoid making eye contact during a conversation in the American context, it might be perceived as a sign that you are distracted or not interested in what the other person is saying, or some people might even perceive it as a lack of confidence or self-assurance. This can also be observed in other WEIRD contexts, as people who maintain eye contact are often perceived as more credible and sincere (Clough & Duff, 2020).

Japanese people tend to use fewer hand gestures when they express themselves to ensure that communication remains clear and respectful. Some people may also find excessive hand gestures too casual or even disrespectful. Hence, in most cases, people may rely on other non-verbal cues such as facial expressions, tone of voice, usually a lower pitch, and body language to convey their message. On the other hand, in American culture, using hand gestures is often seen as a sign of enthusiasm, confidence, and expressiveness. Hence, Americans tend to use a lot of hand gestures to emphasize points, clarify meanings, and make communication more engaging and dynamic (Clough & Duff, 2020; Uono & Hietanen, 2015).

The direct communication style in WEIRD societies is closely tied to individualism. In these cultures, people are encouraged to express their thoughts, opinions, and needs openly and directly. The emphasis on personal autonomy and self-expression means that individuals are expected to look after their own needs first. This fosters a clear and straightforward communication style to ensure that individual needs and preferences are understood and respected (Park et al., 2012). In contrast, collectivist cultures often prefer indirect communication to maintain harmony and avoid conflict (Merkins, 2018). Although this style of communication is generally well-received in the Asia-Pacific region, it can be interpreted as a sign of discomfort, anxiety, a lack of confidence, or self-esteem in cross-cultural encounters.

On the other hand, in the Asia-Pacific context, speaking loudly with excessive hand gestures and direct eye contact may not be well-received and could be perceived as aggressive or intimidating by some individuals. Then, how should we navigate the challenges posed by communicating in different contexts? Should we abandon our own communication style and adopt a new one? The critical point here is to first deepen our understanding of the differences in communication styles. Since abandoning our own communication style, whether implicit or assertive, would be counterproductive, our goal should be to expand our understanding of the various communication styles influenced by the cultural values and beliefs of different societies. As a result, we can develop the cognitive flexibility needed to incorporate these styles into our intercultural repertoire, allowing us to 'get off the bus' at any point along the way, regardless of the context.

3.3 Developing a Universally Acceptable Communication Style: Is it Feasible?

As society becomes more globally connected, the ability to communicate across cultural boundaries has become increasingly important. Especially, since globalization has expanded markets, supply chains, and customer bases from diverse cultural backgrounds, all of which require effective communication for successful negotiations, project management, and customer satisfaction. English language proficiency and cross-cultural awareness are essential skills that facilitate these exchanges. While most people begin learning these skills in school, developing a globally acceptable communication style remains an elusive endeavor.

Language is a dynamic and diverse system, shaped by culture, context, and individual perspectives. It reflects the rich and intricate human experience, evolving to adapt to new contexts and influences (Anyichie et al., 2023; Ting-Toomey & Dorjee, 2014). Despite our efforts to communicate effectively, cross-cultural communication can be intricate due to the subtle variations in behavior and communication specific to different groups or cultures. Non-verbal cues play a crucial role in shaping communication patterns, and cultural nuances have a significant impact on them. For instance, gestures and body language that are considered appropriate in one culture may be misunderstood or even found offensive in another. A firm handshake or maintaining direct eye contact, seen as a sign of confidence in Western cultures, might be perceived as aggressive or offensive in certain Asian cultures where implicit communication is the norm (Uono & Hietanen, 2015). These differences can impact cross-cultural interactions negatively.

In this regard, education plays a critical role in raising awareness of these differences. As we emphasized, we may not be able to encapsulate the whole universe in one word. Yet, it is within the realm of possibility to develop a communication style that is universally acceptable. The first step to accomplish this endeavor in language classrooms is to raise students' awareness of the differences in communication styles and why they would need to adapt to those differences as they engage in intercultural communication. This is crucial, as many Japanese students tend to assume that the implicit and non-confrontational communication style they are accustomed to will be accepted worldwide. Similarly, students from WEIRD contexts may believe their assertive style will be well-received by the Japanese due to the latter's tendency for implicit communication without explicit opinions or comments. However, this assertiveness can sometimes come across as overly aggressive or intimidating, leading to misunderstandings in cross-cultural communication. In this regard, world language classes (used instead of foreign language classes) can serve as an effective platform to raise awareness of these differences and help develop adaptive communication skills through practical training.

Practical training exposes individuals to real-world scenarios where they can practice adapting to new circumstances (Ulanday et al., 2021). For instance, when Japanese students learn the importance of maintaining direct eye contact, using hand gestures, and speaking clearly and confidently in intercultural interactions, they intentionally apply these skills in real-life situations. Similarly, British students studying Japanese practice implicit communication during their interactions in Japanese. When practical training is conducted in groups, individuals practice different communication styles in front of their peers. By observing their peers in action, they can adapt and refine their own communication style (Hooper et al., 2025). When performed regularly, practical training also promotes reflective practice (Egitim & Watson, 2024), providing individuals with the opportunity to reflect on what they have learned and why it matters for improvement. This process further reinforces learning (Bullock & Sanchez, 2021).

Overall, while there may not be a one-size-fits-all approach to intercultural communication, it is possible to develop cognitive flexibility to switch between the two ends of the spectrum (assertive and implicit communication styles) as needed. Achieving this cognitive flexibility is liberating as students can take ownership, adapt to new challenges, and develop solutions to problems in cross-cultural encounters. Thus, language classrooms can serve as an effective platform to raise students' awareness of these different communication styles and the importance of cognitive flexibility. Then, through practical training, students can be exposed to real-life scenarios to apply what they have learned.

3.4 Balancing Communication Styles Through Intercultural Flexibility

As emphasized in the first two sections of this chapter, communication in Japan and other Asia-Pacific countries often relies on an implicit, non-confrontational style, with some variations across these cultures. People frequently understand each other's needs through shared knowledge, non-verbal cues, and subtle hints. This approach helps save face and maintain harmony in social interactions. However, using an implicit communication style can hinder students' ability to effectively convey their ideas during cross-cultural interactions, even if they possess adequate English language proficiency and cross-cultural knowledge. In WEIRD contexts, avoiding eye contact might be perceived as disinterest or a lack of confidence, potentially placing the individual at a disadvantage in the conversation. Speaking softly and minimizing expressive hand gestures during presentations can give the impression that the presenter lacks confidence in their ideas, especially in a multicultural work environment. Hence, we would argue that one needs to develop adaptability in their communication style to manage intercultural encounters effectively.

The question then becomes: How can we help EFL students, who have relied on implicit communication throughout their lives, develop cognitive flexibility? Based on our framework, the first step is to learn the fundamental components of assertive communication to enhance our success in intercultural encounters with people from WEIRD contexts. This includes four key steps: *establishing eye contact, using expressive hand gestures, communicating with a clear and assertive Tone*, and *listening intently* (see Figure 3.1).

The final component, listening intently, refers to paying close attention and actively engaging with what is being said. For instance, in Japanese culture, people often nod to indicate they are listening. However, in WEIRD contexts, this gesture may be misinterpreted as agreement, sometimes leading to confusion. In intercultural encounters with people from WEIRD cultures, it may be more effective to use verbal responses such as 'sure,' 'wow,' 'I see,' or 'hmm, interesting,' and to ask follow-up

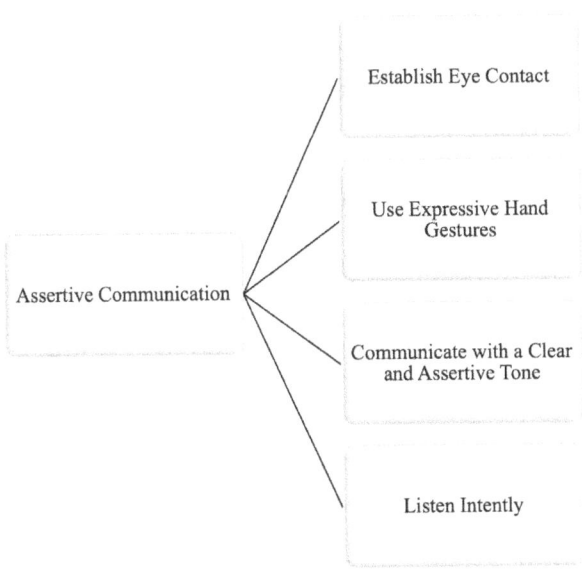

FIGURE 3.1 Assertive Communication

questions to demonstrate genuine interest in the conversation. To effectively incorporate these strategies, regular practice plays an essential role, and English language classrooms provide teachers and students with an ideal setting to enhance the assertive communication style.

Since students primarily practice these four steps in group activities, guidance and support from language teachers and near-peer role models play a critical role. However, we find it necessary to reemphasize that adopting the assertive communication style does not mean abandoning the implicit communication style. Rather, it involves developing the cognitive flexibility to switch between the two styles as needed (Egitim & Sandu, 2023). Let's now delve into the practical side of things and elaborate on the activities we can incorporate to help students develop an assertive communication style, enabling them to successfully navigate intercultural encounters with individuals from WEIRD societies.

One effective way to engage students in oral communication is through presentations, which can be implemented in various formats. First, we suggest having students take turns presenting their weekly homework assignments as a warm-up activity in each class. This approach not only reinforces students' learning but also encourages active participation. Students are divided into groups of three or four, depending on class size, and form a circle to face each other. This setup is important as it allows them to practice making eye contact, observe their peers, and provide feedback on areas for improving their assertive communication style.

Before starting this activity, Japanese students tend to play rock, paper, and scissors to decide who goes first. As part of assertiveness training, we recommend that students practice taking initiative here. Teachers should encourage students in each group to raise their hands and say, 'I will go first,' to take the lead. If two students from the same group raise their hands, they can then play rock, paper, scissors to determine who goes first. Once the first student begins presenting their homework assignment, they are encouraged to establish eye contact with their group members, use expressive hand gestures to emphasize points, illustrate concepts, or convey emotions, and speak with clarity and conviction to engage their peers and encourage active listening. Meanwhile, the other students in the circle observe and take notes to provide constructive feedback. To ensure feedback is actionable and easy to grasp, it is essential to offer structure and scaffolding. Therefore, we recommend using a checklist for this purpose.

The checklist below is designed with student input, following the components of the *leaderful classroom practices* framework presented in Chapter 2 (Egitim, 2021; 2022; Egitim & Umemiya, 2023). Students are provided with the checklist before the presentation starts. After they watch each presenter, they check the appropriate box for each item and add their comment below in the "Additional Points" box (see Figure 3.2). We allow students to write their comments either in English or their native language to help them fully grasp what improvements they need to make and how they should make those improvements. The translanguaging technique enhances the effectiveness of actionable feedback.

Once the presentation of homework assignments is completed, each student reviews the feedback sheets they receive from their peers. After that, students take turns reflecting on what they did well and the areas they need to improve. Incorporating this activity weekly throughout the semester should yield positive results. We believe that by the end of the semester, students should gain awareness of the important role assertive communication plays in intercultural interactions. Some students can already demonstrate the four components of the framework in their communication effectively. However, it is important to recognize that each student has a different pace and our primary goal as educators should be to raise students' awareness of the different communication styles and why they may need to develop cognitive flexibility. Once this awareness is gained, students can gradually master the four steps of our *Global Competence* framework to navigate intercultural encounters (see Chapter 1).

Similarly, we can apply the collaborative peer feedback model to individual and group presentation assignments. In this scenario, each student comes to the podium and gives a presentation

PRESENTATION EVALUATION SHEET	Excellent	To some extent	Needs improvement
Maintained genuine eye contact			
Avoided staring at one person			
Used gestures to emphasize points, illustrate concepts, or convey emotions			
Avoided excessive or distracting hand movements			
Spoke with clarity and conviction			
Pronunciation was clear and articulate			
The tone of the voice was loud enough to be heard by peers			
Spoke at an appropriate speed			
Additional Points:			

FIGURE 3.2 Presentation Checklist

to the whole class. Assigning students this type of presentation task for midterms and finals can be an effective way to determine how much improvement each student has made through the weekly homework assignment presentations in small groups, and provide students with the opportunity to demonstrate what they have learned to a larger audience. Such experience is crucial for students to overcome their fear and build confidence (Kireeti et al., 2024).

The second category in our framework emphasizes the implicit, non-confrontational communication style for people from WEIRD contexts. Take, for instance, the Japanese communication style is often considered high context, a concept introduced by anthropologist Edward T. Hall. In cultures like Japan, messages are conveyed not only through words but also through situational context, behavior, and non-verbal cues. This nuanced approach fosters deeper understanding and connection among interlocutors. In high-context communication, implicit information plays a significant role. This includes shared knowledge, non-verbal cues, and the ability to read between the lines rather than relying solely on explicit verbal messages (Hall, 1990).

One essential aspect of Japanese communication etiquette is *Kuki wo Yomu*, which translates as "reading the air," or "sensing the atmosphere." Before taking action or speaking, individuals assess the unspoken context. This practice helps avoid making others uncomfortable or obligated. It aligns with the idea of *Kao Wo Tateru*, which literally means preserving someone's face or dignity. Essentially, it involves not publicly disagreeing with others to prevent them from losing face. Based on this non-confrontational and implicit communication style, it's essential to practice humility and avoid arrogance (Egitim, 2024). People aim to maintain harmony and show respect by navigating social dynamics with care. Wa (harmony) is a fundamental concept in Japanese culture. Humility and respect play crucial roles in interpersonal interactions. Whether it is using polite language, bowing, or considering others' feelings, the ultimate goal is to promote positive relationships (Jung et al., 2023; Maemura, 2014). For example, people stand to one side in elevators so that those in a hurry can pass without the need to say, 'Excuse me.'

Similarly, on crowded trains, passengers move their backpacks to the front to create more space for everyone so that more people can get on the train.

While such acts of kindness are generally appreciated, they often stem from shared cultural norms. As a result, people from diverse backgrounds may find it difficult to interpret these unspoken gestures without clear guidance. Especially, in classroom settings, where people from diverse cultural backgrounds gather for a shared purpose, conflicts may still arise. For instance, many newly arrived world language teachers in Japan lack Japanese language proficiency due to being able to lead their lives speaking English within English-speaking communities. Hence, they may have difficulty interpreting student behaviors during classroom interactions (Egitim, 2024). Especially, when students prefer to remain silent after being asked a question directly by their world language teacher, this may create tension between the teacher and the student. While the teacher may interpret this silence as rudeness or arrogance, the reality is that silence may convey different meanings. Sometimes students use silence as a face-saving strategy (Nakane, 2012) while in some other cases, they remain silent to indicate that they need help from the teacher (Harumi, 2011).

Direct questioning can indeed make Japanese students feel self-conscious or put them in the spotlight. Most students fear making mistakes in front of others, and in some cases, even if they speak English fluently and are perfectly capable of answering the question, they might prefer to remain silent to avoid standing out. Understanding these unspoken messages, gestures, and expressions can give one a greater advantage in intercultural interactions in Japan. Especially, students from WEIRD contexts, who are supposedly more accustomed to assertive communication could benefit from learning an implicit style to successfully navigate intercultural encounters.

Once again, the question becomes: How can students from WEIRD contexts develop an implicit, non-confrontational communication style? Would that require them to go through the process of unlearning and relearning? The second part of our framework provides a structured approach to grasp this idea. Once again, it is important to emphasize that our goal is not to abandon assertive communication but rather to develop the flexibility to switch between both styles as needed. Our framework proposes five steps to foster implicit communication: navigating shared knowledge and non-verbal cues, reading between lines, maintaining subtle eye contact, speaking softly, and minimizing expressive hand gestures (See Figure 3.3).

Seiko provides practical methods and examples she uses with students from WEIRD contexts. For instance, fostering implicit communicative styles can be incorporated into second language (L2) class activities. One example is teaching specific non-verbal cues, such as back-channeling cues referred to as *aizuchi* in Japanese. These *aizuchi* include frequent nodding or short-spoken response tokens such as *ee* ("yes"), *sodesu ne* ("I see"), or *soudesu ka* ("is that so?"), which can be introduced as useful fillers. The co-author, Seiko, incorporates a session on the use of *aizuchi* and fillers in her beginner-level Japanese classes in the UK. She shows brief video-mediated materials that allow L2 learners to observe contrasting interactions where *aizuchi* are either used

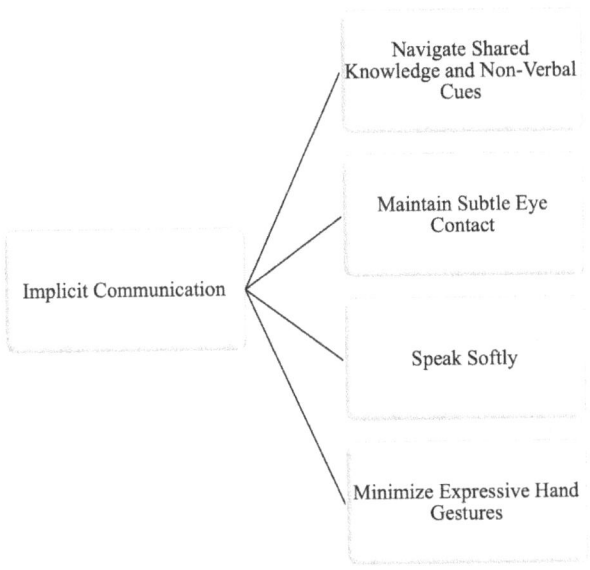

FIGURE 3.3 Implicit Communication

or omitted. The class then discusses how these interactions differ, exploring why they feel natural in some cases and rigid in others. Providing learners with opportunities to observe and reflect on various types of non-verbal communication offers a fresh perspective and serves as a valuable pedagogical approach to raising intercultural awareness while enriching their interactional repertoires. This session typically takes place before L2 learners communicate with native speakers in visitor sessions, as discussed in Chapter 6. It helps learners focus on the use of non-verbal cues, both as speakers and listeners, by engaging their observation and discovery skills. Through this process, learners can better understand, share, and apply knowledge of culturally unique forms of social interaction.

As we demonstrated in the examples, the implicit style would be useful for anyone who intends to engage in cross-cultural communication within the Asia-Pacific context. However, it is important to note that implicit communication, collective identity, and consensus-building are common features influenced by Confucianism. The degree of non-confrontation in communication styles may vary depending on the context (Matsuyama et al., 2019; Richter, 2022; Zhang & Bournot-Trites, 2021). Therefore, adaptability to navigate between assertive and implicit styles is essential for successful cross-cultural communication.

3.5 Conclusion

In Chapter 3, we discussed effective cross-cultural communication in today's globalized world, where interactions span diverse cultural contexts. We emphasized that developing a communication style that balances assertiveness with subtlety is an integral part of achieving successful intercultural exchanges. While English language proficiency and cross-cultural awareness are essential, these two components must be complemented by the ability to navigate the nuances of communication, including non-verbal cues and cultural expectations. Teachers play an important role in guiding students, and regular practice with peers can help raise awareness of varying communication styles and provide practical training opportunities to develop these skills in classroom settings (Egitim & Umemiya, 2023).

For students from the Asia-Pacific region, embracing assertive communication—such as establishing eye contact, using expressive hand gestures, and speaking confidently—can help them engage more effectively with individuals from WEIRD cultures. On the other hand, students from WEIRD cultures may need to learn to appreciate and adopt implicit communication, such as reading between the lines and maintaining harmony, which are vital in Asia-Pacific cultures. These skills are not mutually exclusive; rather, they are complementary, allowing individuals to switch between styles depending on the cultural context and specific interaction.

Through regular practice, reflection, and feedback in language classrooms, students can develop cognitive flexibility and learn to succeed in intercultural encounters. This approach can be empowering for students to take ownership of their communication skills, adapt to new challenges, and contribute to creating more inclusive and effective global interactions. Ultimately, fostering intercultural flexibility and understanding equips individuals to navigate the complexities of our interconnected world, promoting cooperation, mutual respect, and successful communication across cultural boundaries.

References

Anyichie, A. C., Butler, D. L., Perry, N. E., & Nashon, S. M. (2023). Examining classroom contexts in support of culturally diverse learners' engagement: An integration of self-regulated learning and culturally responsive pedagogical practices. *Frontline Learning Research*, *11*(1), 1–39. https://doi.org/10.14786/flr.v11i1.1115

Bowe, H., Martin, K., & Manns, H. (2014). *Communication across cultures: Mutual understanding in a global world* (2nd ed.). Cambridge University Press. https://doi.org/10.1017/CBO9781107445680

Bullock, D., & Sanchez, R. (2021). *How to communicate effectively with anyone, anywhere: Your passport to connecting globally*. Red Wheel/Weiser.

Clough, S., & Duff, M. C. (2020). The role of gesture in communication and cognition: Implications for understanding and treating neurogenic communication disorders. *Frontiers in Human Neuroscience*, *14*(1), 1–22. https://doi.org/10.3389/fnhum.2020.00323

Egitim, S. (2021). Collaborative Leadership in English language classrooms: Engaging Learners in Leaderful Classroom Practices. International *Journal of Leadership in Education*, 28(5), 1–21. http://dx.doi.org/10.1080/13603124.2021.1990413

Egitim, S. (2022). *Collaborative leadership through leaderful classroom practices: Everybody is a leader.* Candlin & Mynard e-publishing. https://doi.org/10.47908/22

Egitim, S. (2024). Does language teachers' intercultural competence influence oral participation in EFL classrooms?: Unveiling learner perspectives through a mixed methods inquiry. *Journal of Multilingual and Multicultural Development*, 1–34. https://doi.org/10.1080/01434632.2024.2306169

Egitim, S., & Sandu, R. (2023). Intercultural language education through leaderful pedagogy: A collaborative autoethnographic approach. In S. Egitim & Y. Umemiya (Eds.), *Leaderful classroom pedagogy through an interdisciplinary lens* (pp. 171–185). Springer Nature. https://doi.org/10.1007/978-981-99-6655-4_10

Egitim, S., & Umemiya, Y. (2023). *Leaderful classroom pedagogy through a multidisciplinary lens: Merging theory with practice.* Springer Nature. https://doi.org/10.1007/978-981-99-6655-4

Egitim, S., & Watson, D. (2024). Language teacher's pedagogical transformation through a critical autoethnographic lens. *Social Sciences and Humanities Open*, 9(1), 1–7. Elsevier. https://doi.org/10.1016/j.ssaho.2024.100837

Gudykunst, W. B., Matsumoto, Y., Ting-Toomey, S., Nishida, T., Kim, K., & Heyman, S. (1996). The influence of cultural individualism-collectivism, self-construal, and individual values on communication styles across cultures. *Human Communication Research*, *22*(4), 510–543. https://doi.org/10.1111/j.1468-2958.1996.tb00377.x

Hall, E. T. (1990). Unstated features of the cultural context of learning. *The Educational Forum*, *54*(1), 21–34. https://doi.org/10.1080/00131728909335514

Harumi, S. (2011). Classroom silence: Voices from Japanese EFL learners. *ELT Journal*, *65*(3), 260–269. https://doi.org/10.1093/elt/ccq046

Hooper, D., Egitim, S., & Hofhuis, J. (2025). Exploring the impact of near-peer role modeling on learners' basic psychological needs: Insights from English classes in Japanese higher education. *International Journal of Educational Research Open*, *8*(1), 1–12. https://doi.org/10.1016/j.ijedro.2024.100429

Jerath, K. S. (2021). Introduction to cross-cultural communication. In K. S. Jareth (Ed.), *Science, technology, and modernity* (pp. 123–145). Springer Nature. https://doi.org/10.1007/978-3-030-80465-7_9

Jonasson, C., & Lauring, J. (2012). Cultural differences in use: The power to essentialize communication styles. *Journal of Communication Management*, *16*(4), 405–419. https://doi.org/10.1108/13632541211279030

Jung, Y., Kim, S., & Tanikawa, T. (2023). Toward a conceptualization of kuuki-wo-yomu (reading the air) in the Japanese organizational context. *Culture and Organization*, *29*(4), 336–355. https://doi.org/10.1080/14759551.2023.2185780

Kreeti, K., Egitim, S., & Thomson, B. J. (2024). Utilizing peer evaluation as a collaborative learning tool: Fostering autonomy satisfaction in English presentation classes. *Language Learning in Higher Education*, *14*(2), 379–400. https://doi.org/10.1515/cercles-2024-0037

Maemura, Y. (2014). Humor and laughter in Japanese groups: The kuuki of negotiations. *Humor*, *27*(1), 103–119. https://doi.org/10.1515/humor-2013-0049

Matsuyama, Y., Nakaya, M., Okazaki, H., Lebowitz, A. J., Leppink, J., & Van der Vleuten, C. (2019). Does changing from a teacher-centered to a learner-centered context promote self-regulated learning: A qualitative study in a Japanese undergraduate setting. *BMC Medical Education*, *19*, 152. https://doi.org/10.1186/s12909-019-1550-x

Merkin, R. S. (2018). *Saving face in business: Managing cross-cultural interactions*. Springer Nature. https://doi.org/10.1057/978-1-137-59174-6

Nakane, I. (2012). Silence. In C. B. Paulston, S. F. Kiesling, & E. S. Rangel (Eds.), *The handbook of intercultural discourse and communication* (pp. 158–179). Wiley. https://doi.org/10.1002/9781118247273

Park, H. S., Levine, T. R., Weber, R., Lee, H. E., Terra, L. I., Botero, I. C., Bessarabova, E., Guan, X., Shearman, S. M., & Wilson, M. S. (2012). Individual and cultural variations in direct communication style. *International Journal of Intercultural Relations*, *36*(2), 179–187. https://doi.org/10.1016/j.ijintrel.2011.12.010

Pipas, M. D., & Jaradat, M. (2010). Assertive communication skills. *Annales Universitatis Apulensis: Series Oeconomica*, *12*(2), 649. https://doi.org/10.29302/oeconomica.2010.12.2.17

Richter, N. E. (2022). An investigation of learning English as a second language in Korea. *Journal of Problem-Based Learning*, *9*(2), 77–86. https://doi.org/10.24313/jpbl.2022.00199

Singhal, A., & Nagao, M. (1993). Assertiveness as communication competence: A comparison of the communication styles of American and Japanese students. *Asian Journal of Communication*, *3*(1), 1–18. https://doi.org/10.1080/01292989309359570

Ting-Toomey, S., & Dorjee, T. (2014). Language, identity, and culture: Multiple identity-based perspectives. In T. M. Holtgraves (Ed.), *The Oxford handbook of language and social psychology* (pp. 27–45). Oxford University Press. https://doi.org/10.1093/oxfordhb/9780199838639.013.013

Ulanday, M. L., Centeno, Z. J., Bayla, M. C., & Callanta, J. (2021). Flexible learning adaptabilities in the new normal: E-learning resources, digital meeting platforms, online learning systems, and learning engagement. *Asian Journal of Distance Education*, *16*(2), 1–5. https://asianjde.com/ojs/index.php/AsianJDE/article/view/580

Uono, S., & Hietanen, J. K. (2015). Eye contact perception in the West and East: A cross-cultural study. *PLOS ONE*, *10*(2), e0118094. https://doi.org/10.1371/journal.pone.0118094

Wierzbicka, A. (2010). Cross-cultural communication and miscommunication: The role of cultural keywords. *Intercultural Pragmatics*, *7*(1), 1–33. https://doi.org/10.1515/iprg.2010.001

Wilczewski, M., & Alon, I. (2023). Language and communication in international students' adaptation: A bibliometric and content analysis review. *Higher Education*, *85*(6), 1235–1256. https://doi.org/10.1007/s10734-022-00888-8

Wilson, D., & Kolaiti, P. (2017). *Implicitness: From lexis to discourse.* John Benjamins. https://doi.org/10.1075/pbns.276

Zhang, H., & Bournot-Trites, M. (2021). The long-term washback effects of the National Matriculation English Test on college English learning in China: Tertiary student perspectives. *Studies in Educational Evaluation*, *68*, 1–21. https://doi.org/10.1016/j.stueduc.2021.100977

4

From Conflict to Mutuality Adopting Values Beyond Our Horizon

Soyhan Egitim and Seiko Harumi

4.1 Beyond Ethnocentrism: Understanding Cultural Fluidity and Inclusive Communication

In the previous three chapters, we discussed the importance of viewing English language education and intercultural communication as interconnected and mutually supportive processes. We also emphasized the value of intercultural encounters in fostering curiosity about others, which should spark a desire to learn more about them and gain new insights. In this way, the new knowledge becomes more meaningful, which may fuel our desire to explore other cultures further. In our third component, we highlighted the importance of developing cognitive flexibility to adapt our communication styles based on the context, which can enhance the success of intercultural interactions. For instance, when interacting with people from Western, Educated, Industrialized, Religious, and Democratic (WEIRD) backgrounds, adopting a more assertive communication style may be effective, whereas shifting to a more indirect style might be more appropriate in the Japanese context. That said, culture and identity are fluid, dynamic constructs that continuously evolve based on experiences, environment, and personal growth (Matsumoto & Hwang, 2013; Vedder & Phinney, 2014). Recognizing the fluidity of these constructs helps us develop a more personalized approach and see individuals beyond generalized cultural or identity markers. This goes for both majority and minority group members in society. Cultural identity is shaped by personal experiences, social contexts, and other factors that go beyond group affiliation. By recognizing each individual's unique experiences and backgrounds, we can move beyond generalizations, misconceptions, and biases, fostering an inclusive environment where everyone's diverse identities and perspectives are valued and respected.

When we are in a majority-group environment as a minority-group member, deconstructing culture and identity can also help us avoid ethnocentric perceptions. By recognizing that cultural and ethnic identities are fluid and context-dependent, individuals can challenge the tendency to view other cultures through the narrow lens of their own (Tajfel & Turner, 1986; Verkuyten, 2005). This process fosters greater empathy and understanding, allowing minority-group members to engage with diverse perspectives and break free from ethnocentric assumptions (Brown, 2010). Ethnocentrism refers to the belief or attitude that one's own culture, ethnicity, or group is superior to others (LeVine & Campbell, 1972). In this regard, people tend to view other cultures or groups from the perspective of their own cultural framework and evaluate other cultures or social groups based on the dominant or familiar culture. As we highlighted in Chapter 1, this ethnocentric perception may manifest during study-abroad experiences. Many Japanese students assume that if they are dissatisfied with certain conditions in their homestays, they should report it to their teacher, who will then pass the message on to the course coordinator. From there, the message will be forwarded to the person in charge of homestays, and eventually, it will reach the host families. This is the typical path a Japanese student would take to avoid unnecessary conflict within the Japanese context. However, in a Canadian homestay, this approach might not be well-received, as most Canadians prefer direct communication. Some may even perceive this implicit style as a two-faced attitude exhibited by students and feel betrayed. Such was the case as we demonstrated in Chapter 1. Then, how can we overcome cultural conflicts fueled by ethnocentric perceptions and move toward mutual tolerance and acceptance of each other? The answer lies in understanding why conflicts arise in intercultural encounters and recognizing how they may be an essential part of developing an introspective and empathetic perspective.

4.2 The Role of Conflict in Intercultural Interactions

Intercultural interactions often involve differences in values, beliefs, and communication styles, which can lead to conflict (Gudykunst & Kim, 2003; Ting-Toomey, 1999). However, conflict in these contexts is not inherently negative. In fact, it can be a vital force in shaping and strengthening intercultural relationships. As individuals navigate cultural differences, the process of resolving misunderstandings can foster greater empathy, enhance awareness of diverse perspectives, and improve communication skills. The sources of intercultural conflict typically stem from those divergent values, communication styles, and perceptions. When these differences are not understood or addressed, they can result in misunderstandings and tension. Therefore, it is crucial to explore the potential sources of intercultural conflict and consider how conflict can be transformed into a powerful tool for both personal and collective growth.

4.2.1 Understanding the Sources of Intercultural Conflict

As we have emphasized, conflict is an inevitable aspect of intercultural encounters. However, to deepen our understanding, it would be helpful to unpack the sources of conflict. Needless to say, cultural differences can greatly influence how actions and words are perceived. What might be considered polite, respectful, or normal in one culture could be viewed as rude, confusing, or inappropriate in another. For example, in cultures with strict adherence to punctuality, like Germany or Japan, arriving late could be seen as disrespectful. In more relaxed cultures, like in some parts of Latin America, arriving late is more acceptable and often expected. As we illustrated with the female Japanese student's shower story in a Canadian homestay earlier in Chapter 1, showering is perceived in Japanese culture as a long and relaxing activity, where people take their time and often enjoy soaking in hot baths. However, in other cultures, the approach to showering may differ. For example, in Canada, people often view showering as a quick, practical activity, typically done right after waking up to refresh themselves in the morning. As a result, if a Japanese student spends more time in the shower than an average Canadian, it may frustrate a Canadian host mother and potentially lead to an intercultural conflict, as was the case in that story.

Furthermore, cultures vary in how they communicate. High-context cultures (such as Japan) rely on non-verbal cues and implicit messages, while low-context cultures (like the United States) emphasize direct, explicit communication (Hall, 1976; Gudykunst & Kim, 2003; Triandis, 2019). For instance, in Western societies where individualist values prevail, people often speak their minds. In contrast, in East Asian cultures like Japan, people tend to communicate subtly and indirectly to maintain harmony. As a result, when a Japanese student goes to study abroad and stays with a host family in the U.S., they are likely to experience misunderstandings due to the differences in communication styles, as we illustrated in our shower and sandwich stories in Chapter 1. In the shower story, the host mother directly expresses her concerns about the student spending too much time in the shower and wasting water. This directness shocks the student, who is unaccustomed to such blunt communication, and the next day, she cannot help but cry.

As we emphasized earlier, ethnocentrism can fuel conflict when interacting with people from different cultural backgrounds. When people view their own cultural norms as 'right' or 'normal,' they may misinterpret behaviors from other cultures. For example, while establishing direct eye contact is perceived as respectful in many Western cultures, it may be considered rude or aggressive in some Asian cultures. Individuals with ethnocentric perspectives may judge these differences negatively, leading to conflict and tension. Ethnocentrism can lead to stereotypes and hasty assumptions about other cultures, as individuals assess others' behaviors and attitudes through the lens of their own cultural norms. For instance, someone who values punctuality might perceive another person's more flexible approach to time as irresponsible instead of interpreting it as a cultural difference. In a business setting, a Japanese person might perceive someone from a more individualistic culture, such as the U.S. or Western Europe, who openly expresses personal opinions or challenges authority as confrontational or inconsiderate, without recognizing that in these cultures, individual expression is valued and encouraged.

Furthermore, power dynamics, often influenced by historical or political factors, can contribute to intercultural conflict (Rumbaut & Portes, 2001; Saaida, 2023). For example, a dominant culture imposing its language, values, or norms on a marginalized culture may create resentment or feelings of inferiority. During the colonial era, British authorities often imposed English as the dominant language for education, administration, and commerce in African and Asian countries. This suppressed local languages and cultural practices and brought a sense of cultural inferiority to the colonized populations (Drelichman et al., 2021; Saaida, 2023). Many were made to feel that their native languages and traditions were less valuable or even 'backward' compared to those of the colonizers. Today, the impact of this dynamic still lingers as post-colonial societies continue to navigate a complex relationship with English and Western influences. This often creates cultural tension and conflict.

Inherent differences in values and social norms, ethnocentric perspectives, and power imbalances between people all play a role in intercultural conflicts. However, it is important to acknowledge that these differences cannot be settled overnight, and it is also debatable whether they need to be settled. We may need to treat conflict as a natural part of the process of coming to resolutions in intercultural encounters so that we can learn to develop empathy, tolerance, and acceptance toward one another.

4.2.2 Impact of Conflict on Intercultural Relationships

In this chapter, we aimed to highlight that intercultural encounters are prone to conflict due to inherent differences in values, communication styles, and worldviews. However, conflict itself is not inherently negative; it often provides a pathway for learning, adaptation, and personal growth in long-lasting intercultural interactions, such as those that take place in school or workplace settings. Working through conflicts offers an opportunity for people to learn about each other's cultures, and over time, it has the potential to promote understanding and empathy among different cultural groups (Egitim & Akalyski, 2024).

Cultures vary widely in how they express disagreement and emotions (Bennett, 2017; Hareli et al., 2015). Working through conflict helps people recognize and adapt to these differences. For example, let's imagine Australian and Japanese students working together on a project and encountering a disagreement during their group work. The Australian students might feel frustrated by the Japanese students' indirectness, interpreting it as evasiveness. On the other hand, the Japanese students might feel uncomfortable with the Australians' directness, fearing it could disrupt harmony and the group dynamic. By working through the conflict, both groups can learn more about each other's cultural backgrounds and communication preferences. The Australian students might come to understand the importance of maintaining group harmony in Japanese culture and adjust their communication style to be more nuanced and respectful. Similarly, the Japanese students might appreciate that the Australians' directness is not meant to be confrontational but rather a way to express differing opinions clearly. This process of recognizing and adapting to each other's communication styles can foster mutual understanding and stronger collaboration, while also enhancing the cognitive flexibility of students and helping them become more accepting and tolerant of one another. Furthermore, as people work through their differences, they often find common ground in shared values, such as respect, honesty, or fairness, regardless of cultural origin. This can be a powerful reminder of our common humanity, reinforcing the idea that while cultures differ, many fundamental human experiences and desires are universal (Bennett, 2017).

Let's imagine a classroom with students from different cultural backgrounds working together on a group project. One student is from Japan, another from Turkey, and a third from Canada. Each student brings their own unique cultural approach to communication, teamwork, and problem-solving. During the group discussions, the Canadian student expresses their ideas directly, encouraging the group to focus on getting the work done quickly. The Turkish student, on the other hand, values building personal connections with their peers first and suggests taking time to get to know each other before diving into the project. The Japanese student prefers a more structured approach, proposing that the group follow a clear plan and reach a consensus before moving forward with any decisions.

At first, these different approaches led to misunderstandings and frustration. The Canadian student may feel that the group is wasting time, the Turkish student may feel uncomfortable with the lack of personal interaction, and the Japanese student may feel that the group's decision-making process is too rushed and chaotic. However, as they work through these differences, the students begin to identify shared values such as *respect* (for each other's ideas and working styles), *honesty* (in expressing concerns openly), and *fairness* (in ensuring everyone's voice is heard). For example, the Canadian student learns to appreciate the Turkish student's emphasis on relationship-building as a way to foster trust within the group, while the Turkish student recognizes the Japanese student's desire for structure and consensus as a means to ensure everyone is equally involved in decision-making. In turn, the Japanese student sees the value of the Canadian student's urgency and clear communication in helping the group stay focused and make progress. Through this process, the students learn to balance their different approaches and find a way to collaborate effectively. This experience helps them understand that despite their cultural differences, their shared values—respect, honesty, and fairness—allow them to work together harmoniously. It reinforces the idea that, while cultures may differ, many fundamental human values are universal, fostering both understanding and cooperation in a school setting. As this conflict-resolution process is repeated over time, it can strengthen long-term relationships and teamwork.

Intercultural interactions, even when initially challenging due to differences in communication styles and values, can lead to valuable learning experiences. By recognizing and adapting to each other's cultural norms and perspectives, individuals can uncover shared human values, such as respect, honesty, and fairness. These shared values provide a common ground that fosters mutual understanding, collaboration, and empathy. In the context of a school setting, this process not only strengthens relationships among students from diverse backgrounds but also contributes to a more inclusive and harmonious environment where all students can work together effectively despite their cultural differences.

4.3 Learning New Values Through Conflict-Resolution Dynamics

Without conflict, it would be difficult to learn new values, as we would exclude ourselves from the process of reflection, adaptation, and growth. In the absence of conflict, individuals may have a tendency to maintain a limited or one-sided view of the world, where they simply reinforce their existing cultural norms and values. However, when conflicts arise, whether in communication styles, expectations, or values, these moments push individuals to engage with and reconsider the values of others. Through this process, people not only learn about the cultural perspectives of others but also become more adaptable, empathetic, and open-minded (Huang, 2023; Huang & Lian, 2023).

Let's revisit the shower situation in the Canadian homestay to remind you of the story and the importance of conflict in learning new values. One day, our student was taking a shower in the evening, just as she would normally do in her Japanese home. All of a sudden, the host mother started knocking on the bathroom door which caught the student by surprise. She quickly finished her shower and left the bathroom, only to run into her host mother on the stairs. The host mother said, "Your showers are too long, and you seem to be wasting a lot of water. From now on, could you limit them to five minutes?" The student was shocked by how directly the host mother had asked her to shorten her shower time. This small cultural conflict made the student reflect on her perception of showering, and the direct communication style of the host mother, and she later shared this story with her teacher, who was chaperoning the group in Canada (Soyhan). The teacher then told all the students that people in Canada generally like to speak their minds directly. Therefore, if you want to successfully adapt to Canadian culture, you may want to embrace this value.

A few weeks later, the teacher walked into the classroom during lunchtime while the students were eating the lunches prepared by their host families. He asked them what they were having for lunch, and many students complained about eating sandwiches every day. The teacher then asked what he could do about it since he was not the one who had made their sandwiches. The students looked at him in surprise, assuming he would "read the air." However, instead, he asked, "What did I tell you about Canadians a few weeks ago?" After thinking for a moment, one student replied, "Canadians like to speak their minds directly?" The teacher smiled and said, "That's right. So, if you want to successfully adapt to this environment, you should also learn to speak your mind directly. You should go to your host family tomorrow and ask them to make you a warm meal for lunch. Of course, be polite with your request, but remember to speak your mind directly." The teacher taught them how to ask for it politely, and the next day, the students who had spoken their minds directly were provided with their warm meals.

There are several key takeaways from these stories. Successful adaptation to a new culture often requires adjusting our behavior and communication style. While this may feel uncomfortable at first, embracing these changes can lead to better integration and improved interactions within the new cultural context. Conflict, particularly when cultural differences arise, offers an opportunity for individuals to reflect on themselves and overcome ethnocentric perspectives, biases, and prejudices. The student's initial shock at the host mother's directness led to reflection, which was a key moment in her learning process. This kind of reflective thinking is essential for personal growth in intercultural settings. Furthermore, by taking the teacher's advice and speaking directly to their host families, the students were able to meet their needs in a culturally appropriate way. This demonstrates how applying the lessons learned from cultural conflicts can lead to real learning outcomes, growth, and greater adjustment to the new cultural environment.

The significance of understanding other cultural values and communication styles was also evident among students from WEIRD contexts who had direct contact with Japanese culture during their study abroad. One notable Japanese cultural value, *honne* (true feelings) and *tatemae* (surface expression), can often pose challenges for students from WEIRD cultural backgrounds, where expressing direct or individual opinions is considered integral to their communication styles and values. In contrast, *tatemae* expressions are often characterized by ambiguous, indirect, or highly routinized and formulaic communication in Japanese contexts. For example, some non-Japanese students perceive the routinized expressions in training manuals encountered at convenience stores as colder in tone compared to the casual small talk common in English-speaking countries, which often includes personalized comments or references to shared, immediate experiences in specific contexts. The co-author, Seiko, experienced the opposite as a former Japanese international student, finding the casual chat in local supermarkets or elevators in British contexts relaxing and refreshing. Such personal, everyday experiences and self-reflection on one's reactions or feelings can illuminate the different cultural values underlying specific communication styles. For WEIRD students, these day-to-day encounters can create feelings of social exclusion, as they may struggle to cross an invisible boundary to fully integrate and feel like members of the host community.

One pathway to achieving a genuinely deeper mutual understanding involves sharing these experiences through conversation. Seiko frequently found this to be a positive learning resource during her time as a non-Anglophone international student, particularly when she encountered difficulties or was driven by curiosity.

Opportunities to share personal experiences, whether inside or outside the classroom, significantly enhance mutual understanding. For example, one British Japanese language learner shared an experience where a social barrier was lowered in a Japanese context. He participated in a school festival where Japanese students engaged openly with others, focusing on fully enjoying the festival rather than adhering to surface-level social interaction patterns. This student's experience highlights how immersing oneself in diverse social contexts can reveal alternative dimensions of interaction specific to those settings. It also demonstrates how such contexts can help individuals cross social boundaries and share genuine enjoyment in social interactions. This theme is explored further in an international student's reflection on different cultural contexts in Chapter 6.

4.4 Steps to Integrating Values Beyond Our Horizon

First and foremost, we do not intend to propose a linear path to adopting new values beyond our horizons. Rather, our goal is to raise awareness of the process individuals may experience. By doing so, we can better envision what it might take to develop the cognitive flexibility needed to thrive in unfamiliar environments. The four steps—*Navigate Cross-Cultural Conflict, Recognize New Values, Acknowledge Differences Through Reflection,* and *Add New Values to Your Intercultural Repertoire*—outline an inclusive and dynamic approach to incorporating new values into existing cultural frameworks (see Figure 4.1).

In multicultural learning environments, navigating cross-cultural conflict is not just about resolving differences—it's about embracing them as learning opportunities. If we start seeing

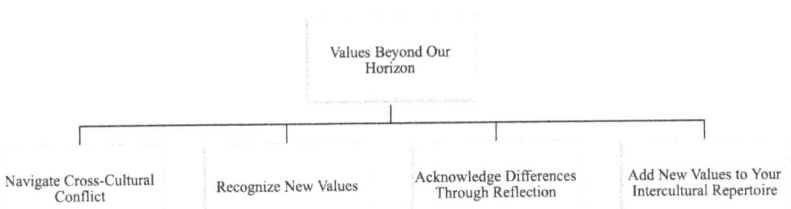

FIGURE 4.1 Adopting Values Beyond Our Horizon

conflict as a natural part of intercultural interactions, we allow ourselves psychological safety to learn from it. As we recognize a different value than our own, we may need to engage in introspection, unpack our backpacks, and recognize our biases and prejudices, which are often shaped by our dominant cultural framework (Egitim, 2025; Franklin, 2014). As we evaluate the influence of new values, we can find a harmonious way to integrate them without losing our own cultural integrity. Once we transcend our ethnocentric perspectives, we become more open to integrating new values into our intercultural repertoire. As our minds repeat this process, we can gradually develop cognitive flexibility to adapt our attitudes and behaviors to diverse environments.

Let's explore the role of reflective practice in helping individuals blend new values with their own cultural identity. As we emphasized earlier, reflective practice encourages individuals to examine their existing cultural beliefs, values, and assumptions. By identifying these, individuals can recognize which ones are deeply ingrained and which ones may be flexible enough to incorporate new perspectives. For example, a Japanese student may experience a feeling of unease towards a Muslim peer's religious practices, such as wearing a hijab, praying at specific times, or following dietary restrictions like not eating pork. This feeling may not necessarily be rooted in the actions themselves but rather in the student's cultural norms—the values, beliefs, and practices they have internalized through their upbringing, community, or society. If the student was raised in a society where such religious practices are uncommon or unfamiliar, their state of confusion might arise from a lack of exposure to or understanding of these practices. Through self-reflection, they may come to understand that the source of their unease is rooted in the cultural norms and values they have grown up with or internalized, as opposed to the other student's religious practices. By recognizing this, the student can identify areas where they may need to improve on, such as being more open-minded, questioning assumptions, or learning about different cultures and beliefs. Furthermore, when it is made a habit, reflective practice nurtures a growth mindset and encourages individuals to embrace change and view the integration of new values as an opportunity for personal development. Over time, this process enhances their ability to adapt to different cultural environments while remaining true to their own identity.

Reflective practice is a powerful tool that enables individuals to examine, question, and adapt their cultural values in response to new ideas and experiences encountered in intercultural settings. By fostering self-awareness and empathy, individuals can integrate new values into their cultural identity, as demonstrated by real-life examples of Japanese students adapting to unfamiliar environments. Such integration promotes personal growth, adaptability, and the development of *global competence*, equipping students to navigate the complexities of a multicultural world with confidence and effectiveness.

4.4.1 Balancing Cultural Identity and Newly Acquired Values

Cultural identity encompasses the traditions, beliefs, languages, and practices that shape an individual's sense of belonging to a particular group (Mercuri, 2012). Cultural values are often passed down through generations. They serve as a bridge connecting the past, present, and future within a community and create a sense of unity and pride. This transmission occurs through various channels, including families as the primary conduit, community and collective influences, and media (Hajro, 2015; Hall, 1976; Mercuri, 2012).

Families instill values, norms, and traditions in children from a young age through daily interactions, storytelling, and role modeling. Especially, language carries cultural expressions, idioms, and ways of thinking that shape identity and worldview.

In terms of community and collective influence, schools play a role in reinforcing national or cultural values through curricula, literature, and history. Collective activities like festivals, gatherings, or communal decision-making reflect and perpetuate shared values. Furthermore, music, art, and dance embody and express the values of a community, preserving them across generations, while films, books, and social media continue to shape and propagate cultural ideals, adapting them for contemporary audiences.

Balancing cultural identity and newly acquired values often involves navigating a delicate tension between preserving our own roots and embracing the transformative experiences acquired through exposure to different cultures, ideologies, or life circumstances (Phinney, 2003; Schwartz et al., 2010). At first, embracing new values may feel like betraying or losing touch with one's cultural roots. For example, Mei, an international student from Japan, moves to the United States to attend university. In Japan, Mei was raised in a culture that emphasizes group harmony, respect for hierarchy, and modesty in self-expression (Gudykunst & Kim, 2003; King & Harumi, 2020). At her university in the U.S., Mei is encouraged to speak openly in class, share her opinions, and advocate for herself, which is a cultural shift that values individualism and assertiveness. It goes without saying that Mei would struggle to adapt to these new cultural expectations. Speaking up in class feels uncomfortable and even disrespectful to her upbringing, where listening attentively and deferring to authority are considered virtues. Mei might worry that becoming more outspoken could mean losing the humility and respectfulness her family holds dearly.

Over time, Mei begins to find a balance by engaging in an internal examination of her feelings through a conflict-resolution process, allowing her to gain a deeper understanding of the cultural values she was raised with and the new expectations she faces. She reflects on her internal conflict, feeling torn between staying true to her upbringing and adapting to her new environment, and recognizes the need to reconcile these seemingly opposing values. Mei begins by observing how her peers communicate in class and identifying ways to participate in discussions. She experiments with framing her thoughts as suggestions or questions, which allows her to share her ideas without feeling that she is compromising her sense of respect and humility—values deeply embedded in her cultural framework. For example, instead of making bold assertions, she expresses her thoughts using phrases like, "I wonder if we could consider..." or "Could it be possible that...?" Conflict resolution also plays a key role in Mei's internal process. She acknowledges her discomfort and reframes it as a natural part of personal growth. Developing self-compassion, she reminds herself that navigating two cultural frameworks is both challenging and rewarding. Through these steps, Mei creates a communication style that bridges the gap between the assertiveness valued in the U.S. and the respectfulness central to her Japanese upbringing. This approach enables her to succeed in both American and Japanese cultural settings.

Mei's story illustrates several key concepts in the context of cultural adaptation, conflict resolution, and personal growth. Mei's experience highlights how internal conflict (torn between her upbringing and new cultural expectations) can be a powerful driver for personal development. This conflict encourages Mei to critically reflect on her values, beliefs, and identity, leading her to a resolution that reconciles seemingly opposing cultural values. The resolution process is not just about finding a quick solution but involves a series of steps: *acknowledging discomfort, reflecting on underlying causes,* and *experimenting with new behaviors.* Mei's process of reconciling her values shows that conflict is not something to avoid but rather a mechanism through which adaptation and growth can occur. Her ability to create a personal communication style that aligns with both American assertiveness and Japanese respectfulness exemplifies a successful conflict resolution strategy that integrates different cultural expectations. Mei's internal examination of her feelings and actions demonstrates the importance of reflective practice in navigating cultural adaptation. Reflective practice allows individuals to step back and assess their responses, feelings, and values in a given situation (Egitim, 2021; Egitim, 2022; Egitim & Umemiya, 2023). For Mei, reflecting on her discomfort helped her view it as part of a larger process of growth, which in turn allowed her to develop strategies to cope with her internal conflict. Mei's ability to adapt is a direct result of her continuous reflection on her experiences. She does not settle for an initial discomfort, but instead, she actively engages with it to find solutions that align with both her cultural identity and the new values she encounters. This ongoing reflective process enables her to integrate new perspectives without losing sight of her own cultural roots.

4.5 Conclusion

In conclusion, intercultural conflict plays a crucial role in personal growth, fostering empathy, tolerance, and cultural adaptability (Bennett, 2017; Brown, 2010). While cultural differences can lead to misunderstandings, they also provide opportunities for self-reflection on our values and communication styles. By approaching conflict with an open mind and a willingness to learn, we can transform potential tensions into valuable learning experiences that deepen our understanding and promote collaboration. Ultimately, embracing and adapting to the diverse perspectives and values of others allows us to create a more inclusive and harmonious world, where people from different cultures and backgrounds can thrive together (Huang, 2023; Huang & Lian, 2023). Mei's story underscores the importance of 'conflict resolution,' 'reflective practice,' and 'cognitive flexibility' in the process of adapting to a new cultural environment. By reflecting on her discomfort and engaging in a thoughtful conflict-resolution process, Mei is able to navigate the tension between her cultural roots and new expectations. Her story demonstrates that adaptation does not require abandoning her heritage values, but instead, it involves integrating new perspectives while staying grounded in her core beliefs. This approach allows individuals to thrive in diverse cultural settings without losing their sense of identity. In essence, Mei's experience shows that cultural adaptation is a complex and ongoing process, one that requires openness to new ideas, reflective self-awareness, and the ability to reconcile multiple cultural frameworks.

References

Bennett, M. (2017). Constructivist approach to intercultural communication. In Y. Kim (Ed.), *International encyclopedia of intercultural communication: Core theories, issues, and concepts* (pp. 1–9). Wiley. https://doi.org/10.1002/9781118783665.ieicc0009

Bennett, M. (2017). Developmental model of intercultural sensitivity. In Y. Kim (Ed.), *International encyclopedia of intercultural communication: Training theories, issues, and concepts* (pp. 1–10). Wiley. https://doi.org/10.1002/9781118783665.ieicc0182

Bennett, M. (2017). Overview of intercultural training. In Y. Kim (Ed.), *International encyclopedia of intercultural communication: Intercultural training overview* (pp. 1–11). Wiley. https://doi.org/10.1002/9781118783665.ieicc0178

Brown, R. (2010). *Prejudice: Its social psychology.* Wiley-Blackwell.

Drelichman, M., Vidal-Robert, J., & Voth, H.-J. (2021). The long-run effects of religious persecution: Evidence from the Spanish Inquisition. *Proceedings of the National Academy of Sciences, 118*(33), 1–9. https://doi.org/10.1073/pnas.2022881118

Egitim, S. (2021). Collaborative leadership in English language classrooms: Engaging learners in leaderful classroom practices. *International Journal of Leadership in Education, 28*(5), 1–21. https://doi.org/10.1080/13603124.2021.1990413

Egitim, S. (2022). *Collaborative leadership through leaderful classroom practices: Everybody is a leader.* Candlin & Mynard ePublishing. https://doi.org/10.47908/22

Egitim, S. (2025). リーダーフルな授業実践による協働型リーダーシップ：みんながリーダー！ [*Collaborative leadership through leaderful teaching practices: Everyone is a leader!*]. Candlin & Mynard ePublishing. https://doi.org/10.47908/34

Egitim, S., & Akalyski, P. (2024). Intercultural experience facilitates majority-group acculturation through ethnocultural empathy: Evidence from a mixed-methods investigation in Japan. *International Journal of Intercultural Relations, 98*, 1–12. https://doi.org/10.1016/j.ijintrel.2023.101908

Egitim, S., & Umemiya, Y. (2023). *Leaderful classroom pedagogy through a multidisciplinary lens: Merging theory with practice.* Springer Nature. https://doi.org/10.1007/978-981-99-6655-4

Franklin, Y. (2014). Virtually unpacking your backpack: Educational philosophy and pedagogical praxis. *Educational Studies: A Journal of the American Educational Studies Association, 50*(1), 65–86. https://doi.org/10.1080/00131946.2014.867219

Gudykunst, W. B., & Kim, Y. Y. (2003). *Communicating with strangers: An approach to intercultural communication* (4th ed.). McGraw-Hill.

Hajro, A. (2015). Cultural influences and the mediating role of sociocultural integration processes on the performance of cross-border mergers and acquisitions. *The International Journal of Human Resource Management, 26*(2), 192–215. https://doi.org/10.1080/09585192.2014.922354

Hall, E. T. (1976). *Beyond culture.* Anchor Books.

Hareli, S., Kafetsios, K., & Hess, U. (2015). Group emotional expressions as a signal of norm violations: A comparison of Israeli, German, and Greek groups. *International Journal of Intercultural Relations, 49*, 120–131. https://doi.org/10.1016/j.ijintrel.2015.02.006

Huang, L. (2023). The impact of intercultural conflict on emotional resilience and adaptability in cross-cultural exchanges. *International Journal of Intercultural Relations, 58*(3), 78–92. https://doi.org/10.1016/j.ijintrel.2022.11.003

Huang, L., & Lian, Y. (2023). Understanding cultural conflicts and building emotional intelligence through intercultural engagement. *Journal of Cross-Cultural Psychology, 45*(4), 482–496. https://doi.org/10.1177/0022022121100997

King, J., & Harumi, S. (Eds.). (2020). *East Asian perspectives on silence in English language education.* Multilingual Matters. https://doi.org/10.21832/9781788926751

LeVine, R. A., & Campbell, D. T. (1972). *Ethnocentrism: Theories of conflict, ethnic attitudes, and group behavior.* Wiley. https://doi.org/10.2307/2129223

Matsumoto, D., & Hwang, H. C. (2013). Cultural competence and intercultural communication: A review of the literature. In K. A. B. Becker et al. (Eds.), *Handbook of intercultural communication and cooperation* (pp. 153–173). Springer Nature.

Mercuri, S. (2012). The role of language in cultural identity: Second-generation immigrants in Canada. *Journal of Cross-Cultural Psychology*, *43*(5), 878–895. https://doi.org/10.1177/0022022112443787

Phinney, J. S. (2003). Ethnic identity and acculturation: A meta-analysis and critique. In K. M. Chavira, R. M. González, & C. L. Llamas (Eds.), *The social psychology of identity and intergroup relations* (pp. 11–32). Sage.

Rumbaut, R. G., & Portes, A. (2001). *Ethnicities: Children of immigrants in America*. University of California Press. www.ucpress.edu/books/ethnicities/paper

Saaida, M. B. E. (2023). The role of culture and identity in international relations. *East African Journal of Education and Social Sciences*, *4*(1), 49–57.

Schwartz, S. J., Zamboanga, B. L., & Wang, H. (2010). The role of culture in identity development: A cultural approach to identity in the context of intercultural communication. In W. B. Gudykunst (Ed.), *The SAGE handbook of intercultural communication* (pp. 347–368). Sage. https://doi.org/10.4135/9781071872987

Tajfel, H., & Turner, J. C. (1986). The social identity theory of intergroup behavior. In S. Worchel & W. G. Austin (Eds.), *Psychology of intergroup relations* (pp. 7–24). Nelson-Hall. https://doi.org/10.4324/9780203505984-16

Ting-Toomey, S. (1999). *Communicating across cultures*. The Guilford Press.

Triandis, H. C. (2019). *Individualism and collectivism* (1st ed.). Routledge. https://doi.org/10.4324/9780429499845

Vedder, P., & Phinney, J. S. (2014). Identity formation in bicultural youth: A developmental perspective. In L. N. S. Chirkov & M. F. J. Oishi (Eds.), *The Oxford handbook of acculturation and health* (pp. 317–336). Oxford University Press. https://doi.org/10.1093/oxfordhb/9780199796694.013.003

Verkuyten, M. (2005). *The social psychology of ethnic identity*. Psychology Press.

5

Developing *Global Competence* Through Self and Collaborative Reflections

Seiko Harumi and Soyhan Egitim

5.1 Applying a *Global Competence* Framework to Intercultural Interactions

In Chapter 1, we have unpacked our Four-Step Framework to develop *global competence* by nurturing: 1) *English language proficiency*, 2) *cross-cultural knowledge*, 3) *adaptability in communication styles*, and 4) *values beyond our horizon*. In the previous chapters, we have learned how important it is for us to continue to work on developing language proficiency so that we can use the target language to deepen our understanding and accurately communicate our exact thoughts and opinions. Furthermore, as suggested by many recent studies on intercultural encounters (Eddy, 2022; Fantini, 2018; Holliday et al., 2021; McConachy & Liddicoat, 2022; Spencer-Oatey et al., 2022), advances in cross-cultural knowledge and global perspectives on intercultural interactions can be augmented by our heightened curiosity through observing

DOI: 10.4324/9781003499848-5

how talk-in-interaction occurs across diverse cultures. Cross-cultural interactions can also serve as a springboard for raising our awareness of how cultural values or beliefs are reflected in the language we use in such encounters. This chapter aims to introduce methods for identifying valuable intercultural perspectives through case studies examining the experiences of Japanese learners of English. By referring to seminal texts that have explored *global competence*, Chapter 5 seeks to highlight the fundamental components of intercultural interactions.

5.1.1 Global Perspectives on Intercultural Interactions

First, we discuss four key perspectives on *global competence* in second language (L2) learning drawn from recent studies, with reference to Japanese learners of English language. These perspectives spotlight 1) the integration of culture and language in L2 learning, 2) L2 learners' cultural identities and intercultural awareness within monolingual contexts, 3) intercultural awareness of self and others, and 4) L2 language user agency and positioning in unfamiliar cross-cultural encounters. This discussion is necessarily mindful of the separation of intercultural from interactional competence explored in Chapter 1, which has recently been emphasized by researchers (Egitim & Umemiya, 2023; Fantini, 2018; McConachy & Liddicoat, 2022) in the fields of intercultural communication, world language education (used instead of foreign language education), and pragmatics. Despite continuing efforts to integrate certain elements of intercultural competence within widely used language frameworks such as the Common European Framework of Reference for Languages (CEFR, 2020), the English as a world language curriculum proposed by Eddy (2022), and rubrics of intercultural communication produced for assessment purposes (Sábcgez-Hernández & Maíz-Arévalo, 2022), opportunities for L2 learners to grasp key perspectives on interactional competence or to experience such intercultural encounters in language classroom settings remain limited. This is despite the call for such pragmatic aspects of interaction to be integrated, even at the beginner level, as long ago as the late 1990s (Kramsch, 1998). The concept of intercultural communicative competence has yet to be fully integrated into L2 teaching practices. As a result, many learners remain insufficiently prepared to navigate and take responsibility for intercultural interactions, both in classroom settings and diverse social contexts.

Second, although the concept of *global competence* has been widely addressed in recent years (see Chapter 1), it remains invariably difficult to grasp if one experiences only one culture and speaks only one language (Fantini, 2018). For example, Masui, a Japanese international student studying in America, explained why it was difficult for him to reflect on his cultural identity as Japanese when initially engaging in group discussions with other international students learning Japanese. He said, "I noticed a difference between the two countries; while Japan has only one race and Japanese people are not very aware of race, it is very important for people living in the U.S. to think about their cultural identity" (p. 18). While Masui's cultural awareness is framed by identity issues rather than language use, his intercultural experience within multilingual contexts led him to say, "I will continue my journey to not only accept my own identity and to love being myself but also to find ways that those who have transnational or multicultural identities can live comfortably in Japan" (p. 19).

Resonating with Arasarantnam-Smith and Deardorff's (2023) viewpoint, Masui's voice clearly illustrates how intercultural experiences can help one understand oneself more fully from others' perspectives. As Masui points out, learning a world language such as English in a monolingual context inevitably limits opportunities for L2 learners to be aware of intercultural differences through natural interaction. This is because they have limited access to diverse cultural practices or experiences of crossing borders to communicate with others from diverse socio-cultural backgrounds. This fundamental restriction needs to be considered as a first step for teachers, practitioners, and researchers who work with Japanese learners of English language. Likewise, this restriction inevitably limits opportunities for L2 learners to observe and notice their cultural identities or unique ways of interacting in their second language. For example, interactional style includes how talk and silence in interaction are differently integrated, not only in the target language but also in the learner's own language. Interactional processes can also include invisible turn-taking practice, turn initiation, or implicit use of silence across diverse cultures (Harumi, 2023b). Nevertheless, with advanced technology, widely available online cultural and language exchange opportunities are now common, and Japanese society includes more people from diverse cultural backgrounds. In the future, these types of access to intercultural interactions via partnership programs have great potential to facilitate intercultural interactions across borders in unique ways.

The third and fourth points namely, the importance of being aware of one's own and others' intercultural values or beliefs as reflected in language use, have been highlighted by recent studies (Bennett, 2013; Spencer-Oatey et al., 2022). For example, Spencer-Oatey et al. (2022) introduce internal and external self-awareness, urging us to recognize our culturally shaped interaction styles, values, and beliefs. They further argue that these styles can shape how others interpret our communications, affecting both language and emotion. In relation to this, Eddy (2022) addressed the key role of learner agency, which involves taking responsibility for one's own interactional footsteps along the path of intercultural engagement. Her proposed framework for developing intercultural communicative competence across diverse languages includes the interpretative mode, an observation stage, and the interpersonal-interactive mode, in which interactants from both sides need to negotiate their own interactional styles and their positioning within specific contexts to facilitate mutual understanding. Eddy continuously stresses the need to recognize that "[language] learners are active social agents co-constructing meaning through mediation across language and culture" (Eddy, 2022, p. 15) and "actively interpreting communication and making evaluations of others' pragmatic behaviors" (McConachy & Liddicoat, 2022, p. 7), along with teachers. Using our Four-Step Framework for *global competence* as our foundation, the following section will examine specific cross-cultural challenges encountered by Japanese learners of the English language and how they tackle these interactional issues.

5.1.2 Cross-Cultural Problematic Encounters of Seiko Harumi

In this section, Seiko, one of the authors, explores how people respond to unfamiliar or unexpected intercultural experiences and engage in natural interactions as participants. She discusses the cross-cultural challenges she encountered, all while keeping in mind the four key components of our *global competence* framework and the perspectives on intercultural encounters mentioned earlier. The following is an account of Seiko's own intercultural journey involving forms of address and whether to address someone by their first or last name (with or without a title), which reflects pragmatic variations in specific socio-cultural contexts. (Fantini, 2018).

Seiko:

> *Born in Japan, graduated from a Japanese university with an English major.*
>
> *Work experience: Taught English in Japanese secondary schools and universities and currently teaching Japanese language at a UK university.*

Here, Seiko shares the cross-cultural dilemmas she has encountered in two roles: (1) as a Japanese university student during her short-term study abroad program in the UK and in English language classrooms in Japan, and (2) later as a Japanese language teacher in UK universities. All examples focus on differences in how 'teachers are addressed' in language learning contexts in Japan and the UK. These accounts closely reflect how language was used (the first component of the *global competence* framework) in specific contexts, in relation to the second component (cross-cultural knowledge), and explore how we can better understand other cultures' practices by cultivating curiosity and discovering new perspectives beyond our horizons (Fantini, 2018; Spencer-Oatey et al., 2022).

My Story 1: How shall I address you?

Seiko:

> When I attended a short-term study abroad program to study academic skills in the UK, the first thing I noticed as a Japanese learner of English was the dynamics of classroom interaction and the relationship between teachers/lecturers and students. One fundamental but noticeable difference which surprised me from day one was the way other international students addressed teachers in the classroom. Except in very formal settings in which lecturers were addressed by title, other students were addressing teachers by their first names as they would as friends. English classes with native English speaking teachers where teachers and students addressed each other using first names could be commonplace after some sort of agreement between them, even within Japanese educational contexts. This is rare however, especially in the case of Japanese teachers, even those teaching English, as it is considered somewhat impolite or simply rude to call teachers by their first names, at least in classroom contexts. I initially felt shy to follow this practice. At the same time, I felt a more friendly atmosphere in the classroom, with no strict hierarchical relationship between teachers and learners and a closer psychological distance between them. This practice reminded me of another occasion in an English language class in Japan when one of my classmates addressed an American English lecturer as 'teacher!' (a direct translation of the Japanese word sensei) in English to get her attention, without using her name. Soon after, the teacher replied, 'I am Karen.' Her tone of voice indicated her reluctance to say this, and my classmates and I sensed a tense atmosphere arising from what we heard. I then became aware of my classmate's fundamental pragmatic failure (Thomas, 1983), as seen from a Western perspective, in not addressing our teacher by name and, as Karen might have inferred, as an individual. Yet, from my classmate's perspective,

she had only just transferred the traditional Japanese custom of addressing a teacher as sensei, without using a personal (usually family) name, which is common practice in Japanese educational contexts. In both cases, my fellow Japanese students of English language and I encountered unexpected situations or reactions involving the way we, as students, should or could address teachers in classroom contexts using English. While these experiences were initially unfamiliar and engendered a tense or anxious atmosphere or even hesitation to adopt a new way to address teachers, they made me aware of different educational practices and values, sparking curiosity about the simple but daily procedure of addressing teachers in English. As a teacher of Japanese in multilingual contexts, I often encounter comparable situations. Although I now feel most comfortable addressing my teachers by their first names and being addressed in the same way in English contexts, as a Japanese language teacher, I feel most comfortable being addressed as 'Harumi sensei,' linking my family name with the form of address 'teacher.' This is because it is the formal and widely accepted practice in Japanese educational contexts, which I was accustomed to before encountering new learning contexts involving Western perspectives. I feel uneasy if my students learning Japanese address me as 'Seiko!,' using my first name. This reflects an anecdote about a Japanese boy who moved to the UK at an early age and started addressing his mother by her first name, Chieko. His mother was perplexed by this joyful but inappropriate form of address. Some of my Western students are particularly aware of the importance of Japanese forms of address, which play an integral role in language use and social relationships. These students sometimes ask me in advance which form of address I am most comfortable with, in both Japanese and English. I feel grateful for the cultural sensitivity (Bennett, 2013) with which these students approach this fundamental question, but I am conscious of how this could affect the teacher's identity. I recall my American lecturer Karen, who felt uncomfortable when addressed simply as 'teacher.' As **Fantini (2018)** observes, *"Whether to employ a title, which title to use, or whether to address someone by first or last name (with or without a title) all reflect sociolinguistic variations dependent on perceived relative status and relationships between interlocutors, as determined by culture"* (p. 11). *These incidents, which took place first when I was a student in an English language/academic skills classroom and later when I was a teacher in a Japanese language classroom as a teacher, reminded me of the importance of understanding each culture's practices and values. Although the way we address others may not appear serious at first, these experiences taught me the importance of fostering cross-cultural awareness by imaginatively understanding others' points of view in specific contexts and reflecting on our interpretations, emotional responses, and adaptation to different situations we encounter. I also became aware of limitations when adopting direct, literal translation across different languages or importing my own cultural values in the context of the target language without noticing how others interpreted my intended meanings or reflecting on my expectations for my students to do likewise. How about your learning and social contexts when you learn a new second language? Have you had any uncomfortable or uneasy experiences arising from the ways you are addressed either in your own or a second language in which you are communicating?*

My Story 2: Am I using Aizuchi too frequently or not enough?

Seiko:

Turning to the third approach to developing adaptability in communication styles as a global competence, I experienced a cross-cultural pragmatic failure (Thomas, 1983) *involving transferred Japanese communicative style when interacting in English in the UK. My Japanese listening practices, called aizuchi, which included back-channeling cues or reactive tokens prompted unexpected negative reactions from an English friend. The listener-oriented conversational style in Japanese is characterized by frequent use of aizuchi, which typically involves frequent vertical head nods and/ or short reactive tokens such as 'un/u:::n (uhm)' used to create rhythms in conversation enhanced by constant mutual monitoring using verbal or non-verbal reactive tokens. On the other hand, I also experienced uneasiness when people I was talking to in English seemed to be simply listening as I spoke without responding in any way. Soon after arriving in the UK as an international student, I seized every opportunity to interact in English and tried to use facilitative communication skills as much as possible. From my perspective, this strategy included positive listenership, indicated by using aizuchi, non-verbal reactive tokens. However, on one occasion, after I had been talking to an English friend for a few minutes, he suddenly stopped speaking and said, "You don't have to agree with every single point I make." Upon hearing this genuine but unexpected reaction, I was somewhat shocked to discover that my ideal aizuchi listenership behavior was not interpreted as I had expected. Later, I learned that such misinterpretations have been scrutinized in the field of pragmatics* (Maynard, 1989), *which studies how language and interactional styles differ from one culture to another. It investigates practices such as aizuchi, which act as signals for the speaker to continue, and frequent back-channeling. Critically,* Maynard (1989) *observed that listeners' back-channeling usually occurs during pauses or silences between clausal units of utterance, at the end of a speaker's turns, or simultaneously at any time when they hold the floor to signal attentive listening. This close bilateral monitoring by the speaker and listener can create a rhythm of interaction using non-verbal reactive tokens such as back-channeling or smiles when the listener remains silent* (Kogure, 2007). *A similar concern has also been raised by Japanese learners of English language* (Harumi, 2011), *as revealed by survey responses. These learners expected English language teachers to provide back-channeling cues confirming they understood what they said. Responses to survey questions asking about ways teaching strategies can help students to continue speaking in*

English classes included: 'Offer a back-channeling response when the teacher understands what I want to say,' 'Show a willingness to understand' or 'Display understanding of nonverbal behavior.' According to students, teachers' use of aizuchi in such contexts can make it easier for them to continue conversations or respond in English. In the absence of aizuchi, these learners feel uneasy as they are unsure whether teachers understand them or are interested in listening to what they are saying. I myself experience a similar uneasiness when I receive a few reactive tokens while talking in English. Although I am now accustomed to continuing a conversation in English without receiving frequent reactive tokens, they can nevertheless help me to continue talking in a more positive way. Likewise, referring to the lack of back-channeling behavior in American cross-cultural communication, Maynard (1989) *has pointed out that Japanese people may consider other non-Japanese participants unwilling to cooperate with them in the mutual activity of smoothing out potential differences of opinion. On the contrary, Americans may have negative reactions to what they see as mindless agreement or inappropriate rushing when listeners send frequent reactive token messages within a noticeably short time span. As my experiences illustrate, if the rhythm of interactional styles is not shared among participants, perhaps because they are from diverse cultural backgrounds, "they cannot perform the dance of synchronized rhythmic ensemble well"* (Maynard, 1989, p. 232). *As* Maynard (1989) *points out, what underlies these different characteristics is invisible interactional management in Japanese and English social contexts. Instead of remaining within these silos by using the defined value systems of each community, we should seize every opportunity to heighten awareness, broaden and inform by globally inclusive perspectives* (Spencer-Oatey et al., 2022). *In the case of the fourth step, seeking to nurture 'values beyond our horizons,' communicating from the perspectives of others, what can we do? If you encountered the situation outlined in the following section, how would you respond?*

5.2 The Use of Silence in English Language Classrooms in Japan

The use of silence in the Japanese English language classroom has been a widely discussed topic for several decades due to Japanese EFL learners' silent responses or reticence frequently observed in English classrooms (Harumi, 2011; King, 2013). More specifically, silent or quiet responses following teachers' questions have often been seen as indicators of difficulty in using the language. They have frequently been attributed to learners' difficulty in understanding, expressing their own ideas, and interacting with others to maintain and progress conversation (Harumi, 2023a). Complementing this, a comprehensive study by King (2013), which investigated Japanese university students' silence in the ELT classroom, revealed that learners' silence is also related to their reluctance to initiate classroom interaction.

While initial studies investigating silence in the Japanese English classroom took a negative view of Japanese silence, reflecting a Western perspective that emphasizes verbally-oriented interaction generally seen from teachers and researchers rather than learners' points of view, a study by Harumi (2011) which investigated the reasons for silence and possible pedagogical solutions, focusing on Japanese learners of English language, first language (L1) Japanese-speaking teachers, and L1-English-speaking teachers, revealed multiple explanations for silence, some linguistic and others psychological, socio-cultural, or interactional. Although learners' and teachers' perspectives sometimes overlapped, there were noticeable differences in their respective uses of silence as well as in its causes and the messages it conveyed. On the other hand, recent studies on silence have explored more constructive and positive roles of silence in L2 learning, as seen from diverse perspectives (Bao, 2023; Harumi, 2020; Harumi, 2024). In this section, we explore the role of silence from diverse and inclusive perspectives, firmly situating the language classroom as a place for intercultural encounters.

5.2.1 Case study 1: Silence in the L2 Classroom

In our first case study, we look at part of a video transcription from an English classroom (Harumi, 1999) and different views on the use of silence by Japanese and British participants who watched the video. In this case study, we focus on exploring the phenomenon of silence through observation and analysis and discuss ways in which we would respond to this situation from both the student's and teacher's perspective, exploring the practical steps that can be taken in order to facilitate interaction. This involves taking account of values on silence and talking beyond our horizons, adopting two-directional perspectives. The scope of this case study includes:

- Observation of classroom interaction, in a Japanese context
- Identifying intercultural difficulties experienced in this interaction
- A student's use of silence in interaction
- A teacher's response to students' silence
- Reflecting one's cultural identity through the use of silence in interaction
- Finding ways to facilitate interaction

The case study focuses on a learner's silence after a teacher asks a question in a Japanese English classroom. The teacher is from the USA, and the student's overall proficiency level is lower-intermediate.

Activity 1

Read the questions below first, and then look at the transcription, in which you can see the interaction between an American English teacher and a student in an English class. Answer questions 1 to 6 as fully as possible and then discuss your answers with your classmates. Then engage in role-play with one of your classmates, improvising on the situation outlined in item 7 below, and afterward discuss with this classmate, and possibly others as well, examining different ways to facilitate interaction (see Table 5.1).

TABLE 5.1 *Silence in English Language Classrooms*

T:	So, other examples of … is the best way of … Miss Tanaka (a key sentence has been also written on blackboard)
S:	(7.8) +she hangs her head down and looks blank, complete absence of facial expression
T:	Eating ice-cream is the best way of what?
S:	(11.6) +she looks down but looks at the teacher when the teacher starts saying something
T:	Eating ice cream is the best way to **beat** the **heat**, to **beat** the **heat** (.) do you agree what I mean? (…continues another 4 sentences) Do you agree?
S:	(4.1) +she looks away
T:	**yes**, sir, **no** sir, **I don't know**. **Three** options. **Yes**, **No**, or **I don't know**.
S:	(5.7) °I don't know°

(Harumi, 1999, p. 252)

Guiding questions (A): Observation and analysis of classroom interaction:

1. What was your first impression of this classroom?
2. What is happening in this class? Is communication between the teacher and student proceeding smoothly? Why?
3. In total, how many questions are you asked by the teacher in this interaction?
4. How many verbal answers does the student give?
5. How long does the student usually wait before speaking after the teacher asks a question?
6. How does the student try to communicate non-verbally during silence (e.g., gestures, eye contact, head movement)?
7. How would you interpret the student's silence and non-verbal behavior?
8. According to the script, you can role-play and find out how the student and the teacher feel in this context. You need to observe the length of silence and act out the gestures. You can then share your experiences in this imaginary class.

9. Discuss possible ways to facilitate interaction. What would you do in this context?

*Transcript convention

(.)	Brief silence, less than one second
(0.0)	timed pause (in seconds)
=	next speaker takes turn immediately after the first speaker
WORD	loud sound
° °	quiet sound
:::::	elongation of sound
(( ))	gesture
( )	author's notes
+	indicates the beginning of non-verbal interaction

Activity 2

The transcript in Activity 1, along with the video clip, was shared with two groups of adults. These comprised 10 Japanese and 10 British participants. They shared their interpretation of silence in the classroom by viewing a video of classroom interaction in Activity 1 (see Table 5.2).

TABLE 5.2 *Interpretation of Learner Silence*

Japanese participants	British participants
• She does not want to stand out. • She expects the teacher will shift his attention to other students or give up if she remains silent. • She is waiting for the teacher's help. • She keeps silent since she thinks she can't deal with this situation on her own. • She wants the teacher to realise that she doesn't understand without actually saying so.	• She finds it boring. • She is rude. • She is uninterested and hopes that if she does not answer, the teacher will leave her alone. • She appears lazy as she does not try to understand and when she finally answers, she says 'I don't know' (an easy option). • They apparently not to want to stand out in the group.

Guiding questions on Japanese learner silence from others' perspectives (B):

1. Is your interpretation of silence similar to the ones on the list?
2. Summarize 1) Japanese participants' interpretation of silence and 2) British participants' interpretation of silence. Are there any similarities and differences in the way they view the Japanese learners' silence?
3. Discuss the reason why attitudes towards silence in interaction differ between the two Groups.
4. Why do you think Japanese students mostly respond to questions with silence? Do you think you would reply in the same way or differently? Can you think of other ways to respond to the questions?
5. Speak to your classmates and teacher about what speakers of English may feel when they receive no response in a conversation, and what silence means in English language contexts.
6. What is your view on occasions when you might need more time before responding verbally in an English classroom? How can you let another person know that you need more time?

Reflection 1

Having looked at the transcript of Japanese classroom discussions with your classmates and your teacher, let's reflect on your perceptions of the use of silence (and talk) in relation to your own cultural identity or interactional values and those of British participants. Reflection points are listed below, but you can add more ideas (see Table 5.3):

♦ Silence can be considered positive or negative in my cultural/educational contexts
♦ This is because silence in communication functions and is interpreted as ……
(Please continue)

TABLE 5.3 *Use of Silence*

Silence in Japanese contexts	Silence in British contexts
My understanding of core values on the use of silence are	In English speaking contexts, the value of silence can be considered

Activity 3

Let's look at different ways questions are answered in an American ESL classroom. Pay attention to how the interaction changes when a teacher asks questions and how students respond. Try to identify ways of answering questions that are different from those in a Japanese classroom. When students have difficulty answering, how do they try to resolve the issue? In this context, this type of problem-solving strategy is called 'repair' (*shyufuku*). In the classroom, there are both Japanese students and other international students (see Table 5.4).

TABLE 5.4 *Answering Questions in the American ESL Classroom*

T:	Do you know the expression it's no use crying over spilt milk
S2:	Yes.
S1:	=ah yes I've heard=
T:	=you have heard this?=
S1:	Yes, we have (0.5) a similar saying in Japan=
T:	=aah what is it in Japanese?
S1:	er. [Fukusui bon ni kaerazu] (Spilt water won't go back into its tray). ((The Japanese students say it in Japanese with T attempting to repeat))
T:	and how does that…
S1:	It's no it's no use it's no point, it's no use (1.0) aah=
S3:	=the water which spilt over
S1:	(1.0) over tray?=
S3:	=tray

Topic : It's no use crying over spilled milk.
T: teacher, S1 = student 1, S2 = student 2, S3 = student 3

(Richards, 2006, pp. 65–66, Japanese proverb added in Harumi, 2023a).

Guiding questions on observations and analysis of classroom interaction (C):

1. What is your first impression of this classroom?
2. What is happening in this class? Is communication between the teacher and students proceeding smoothly? Why?
3. In total, how many questions does the teacher ask in this interaction?
4. How many answers are given verbally by the student?
5. How long does the student usually wait to begin speaking after the teacher asks a question?
6. How does the student try to solve communication problems?
7. What kinds of fillers or verbal expressions do the students use?
8. Using the transcript as your starting point, you can role-play and find out how these students and the teacher feel in this context. You can then share your experiences in this imaginary class with those in Activity 1.
9. List the similarities and differences in the way the teacher and students communicate in the classroom in Activity 1 and Activity 2.

Reflection 2

Having looked at the transcripts for the Japanese classroom (Activity 1) and the ESL classroom in America (Activity 3 below), discuss similarities and differences in the way communication progresses and the use of silence and talk. List the ways students answer the questions (e.g., gestures, eye-contact, body shifts, head-movement, use of fillers, and co-operation from other students) (see Table 5.5). Please include:

TABLE 5.5 *Comparative Classroom Observations and Analysis*

Similarities between classes in Activities 1 and 3	Differences between classes in Activities 1 and 3

TABLE 5.6 *Observation on the Use of Repair Strategies*

Interactional resources used in Japanese contexts to reply to questions	Interactional resources used in American ESL contexts to reply to questions

- Similarities and differences in the way communication progresses in the classes in Activities 1 and 3.
- Types of interactional resources used in classes in Activities 1 and 3.

Likewise, Japanese L2 learners need to be encouraged to look at cross-cultural perspectives, helping them to understand how their interactional behavior, inner thoughts, and use of silence, seen as "internal self-awareness," could affect others' emotional reactions (Spencer-Oatey et al., 2022, p. 25) or vice versa. The place of silence in interaction and of values attached to the phenomenon of silence in the Japanese language and culture also need to be addressed and shared, as a learning resource, with those who are unfamiliar with these values (see Table 5.6).

5.2.2 Case Study 2: Study Abroad Contexts and Communication with International Students

In our second case study, we examine the experiences of Kana, a Japanese learner of English language who spent a year in the UK. We explore the cultural and interactional experiences she encountered and how her views and perspectives evolved over the years. Kana's journey can be divided into three stages: upon arrival, the middle stage, and towards the end. These phases illustrate how she adapted her interactions and negotiated her identity as an English learner.

Before we look at Kana's story, as a comparison, an account shared by students from Arabic countries on their arrival at their pre-sessional courses in the UK illustrates their first impressions of studying abroad. What did students expect before coming to the UK and did their initial experience match with their expectations?

Extract 1

My expectations about life in the UK were 180 degrees different. In the first week of my stay in the UK, I thought I would just see British people and my English would. improve automatically by building close relationships with British people and speaking English for 24 hours a day. Unfortunately, none of my flat mates or classmates was British. (Lana's story, Hajar, 2020, p. 228)

Extract 2

When I came to the UK, I expected that my English become like a native speaker's and I'd be acquainted with the British culture after a short period in the UK. I did not know that almost all students attending the pre-sessional course would be from EastAsia...My classmates are Asian and Arab. (Yosef's story, Hajar, 2020, p. 228)

As we can see, these students' expectations of using English when surrounded by British people turned out to be completely different in terms of language use and the people they communicated with. This unexpected situation and the surrounding learning environment can initially present a challenge to learners seeking to explore diverse possibilities to improve their English. However, despite these challenges, many learners actively navigate their environments and adapt their strategies to achieve their goals. This brings us to the question: How do language learners seek ways to fulfill their aspirations to improve their English language proficiency and experience intercultural encounters? Hajar's study (2020) highlights how an initial utopian vision of automatic language development and meaningful interactions with locals upon entering the environment was gradually reshaped and positively mediated by the guidance and support of language tutors, ultimately leading to the achievement of proximal goals, such as improving academic writing skills.

Initially, many language learners harbor the expectation that immersion in an English-speaking environment will automatically lead to rapid improvement, particularly through spontaneous conversations with native speakers. However, Hajar's findings suggest that this idealized vision often does not align with reality. Learners may encounter challenges, such as difficulty in initiating conversations or understanding cultural nuances. In this context, the role of language tutors and near peers becomes crucial. They provide not only linguistic support but also guidance in navigating social and cultural differences, helping learners set realistic, achievable goals (Hooper, 2025). Furthermore, near-peer role models can play a vital role by offering relatable guidance and support. These individuals, often just a few steps ahead in their learning journey, can share practical tips, real-life experiences, and strategies that resonate more closely with learners' current challenges. Near-peer role models also provide emotional support, as their proximity to experience fosters a sense of camaraderie and motivation. With consistent tutoring and near-peer role models (Hooper et al., 2025), learners can shift their focus from abstract language acquisition to more concrete, measurable skills, such as improving academic writing (Kireeti et al., 2024). This process enables students to gain confidence, refine their language abilities, and gradually achieve their proximal goals, leading to a more productive and fulfilling learning experience. As a comparison, we shall now look at the experiences of a Japanese learner of the English language, Kana. By following her interactional trajectories, we can observe both her struggles in intercultural encounters and the facilitative steps she took to improve.

5.2.2.1 Kana's Story- 1

This case study explores Kana's initial intercultural experiences upon her arrival in a rural town in the UK for a year-long English language study abroad program. Kana reflects on her experience:

> *When I came to England for the first time, I was hardly able to speak English, both in class and with my homestay family. With other international students whose English proficiency was also extremely limited, I often used a mobile phone to show images to communicate and point out things, and most verbal exchanges were limited to monosyllabic words despite my previous English language learning experience in Japan. Regarding the host family, who were extremely nice and caring, I felt extremely sorry for them, but because of the language barrier between us, gradually, we talked less and less. During this period, I did not connect to anybody. Nobody knew me, and I did not have any means to express myself either in Japanese or English (Interview 1, translation by the author)* (Harumi, 2024, p. 276).

Activity 1

After reading Kana's story, identify the following: 1) the difficulties she encountered, 2) the communication strategies she used, and 3) how she reflected on her learning environment. Discuss these points with your classmates.

Guiding questions on the initial learning environment during study abroad (A):

1. Who did Kana communicate with during the initial stage of her study abroad? What types of difficulty did she experience?
2. Identify the types of communication strategy she used, including any learning materials and non-verbal communication.
3. What was her psychological state at this stage?

4. Share your opinion about the voice she shared, 'During this period, I did not connect to anybody. Nobody knew me, and I did not have any means to express myself either in Japanese or English'. What did she wish to do?
5. If you were Kana, what would you do for the next step to improve your English?

Reflection 1

Based on the discussions with your friends, summarize what you have learned from Kana's story by listing key facts or ideas (Table 5.7).

TABLE 5.7 *Summaries*

Difficulties experienced	Use of interactional strategies	Next steps to improve English and your recommendations

Activity 2

After three months, Kana began learning to play the guitar with a British guitar teacher. Read the following conversational transcript and discuss the communication strategies she developed over time.

R: How was your guitar lesson?
K: In terms of communication, it was so hard as he is not like my English teacher in class. I could not understand very much at

first. The pace of talk is so fast, and he does not slow down. No special treatment. Also, having observed his reaction such as facial expression, I noticed very often he did not understand what I wanted to say. So, I am under pressure to say something and perhaps, I might have said unnecessary things. In Japanese, I tend to listen and try to use aizuchi (back-channeling) a lot. but in English, the other person must find it difficult to understand me so, I always feel I have to say something.

R: Then, how did you try to improve your communication?
K: I tried to use different expressions as much as I could. It is still difficult but my understanding improved a lot and I am happy with my progress when communicating with him (Interview 4, translated by one of the authors).

Guiding questions on Kana's communication with her British guitar teacher (B):

1. By communicating with her guitar teacher, what did Kana learn about communication in English with an L1-English speaker outside class?
2. When she found it difficult to maintain talk, what did she do? What types of strategies did she use?
3. How does she feel about her communication skills (see Table 5.8)?

Reflection 2

TABLE 5.8 *Summary of Findings from Discussions*

Things Kana learned from communication with L1-English speaker	Communication strategies Kana used to facilitate communication and types of improvement

Activity 3

Upon moving to a large city, Kana developed a close friendship with a student from Saudi Arabia and shared her thoughts about their relationship and communication. After reading her statement, discuss the reasons why they became good friends. Do you think this friendship helped Kana improve her English skills? If so, in what ways?

> *It was the first time I met a Saudi Arabian woman and learned about her vastly different culture. I found the societal roles of men and women particularly fascinating. This distinct difference from my own culture made me extremely interested in talking to her. She, in turn, was curious about Japanese culture, which she had some knowledge of through social media, Netflix, and YouTube"* (Interview 2).

Guiding questions on communicating with international students from Saudi Arabia (C):

1. What did Kana learn about her friend's culture? Why was she interested in her friend's culture?
2. Why do you think they became good friends?
3. What types of Japanese culture do you think other international students are interested in? You can search media resources, such as Netflix or YouTube.
4. Which are your favorite foreign countries and are there particular aspects of their culture you are interested in (see Table 5.9).

Reflection 3

TABLE 5.9 *Sharing Ideas*

Why did Kana become close friends with a student from Saudi Arabia?	What are your recommendations to people interested in learning about Japanese culture?	What are your interests in other cultures?

5.3 Conclusion

In this chapter, we have reflected on a Four-Step Framework for developing *global competence* in intercultural encounters. We began by examining current practices in world language education, with a focus on intercultural competence and intercultural communicative competence, as well as the situation in predominantly monolingual contexts such as Japan. Through anecdotes and case studies, we identified aspects of communication that could lead to misunderstandings or challenges in intercultural encounters. These included, for example, terms of address, the role of talk, silence in interaction, and the use of repair strategies. In these case studies, we observed and analyzed actual classroom interactions in both monolingual and multilingual contexts and listened to the experiences of sojourners in study abroad programs.

The insights gained from these case studies and real-world experiences provide a deeper understanding of the complexities involved in developing *global competence*. By reflecting on how communication practices vary across cultures and recognizing potential areas of misunderstanding, we can better equip ourselves and others to navigate intercultural interactions more effectively. While this chapter has focused on introspective reflection through the experiences of others, the next chapter will explore practical scenarios with real-world implications, highlighting current practices such as cultural-language exchanges and tandem learning. Building on these reflections, it will also offer practical strategies for applying these concepts in everyday language learning and cultural exchanges, further enhancing our ability to foster *global competence* in diverse environments.

References

Arasaratnam-Smith, L., & Deardorff, D. (2023). *Developing intercultural competence in higher education: International students' stories and self-reflection*. Routledge.

Bao, D. (2023). *Silence in English language pedagogy: From research to practice.* Cambridge University Press. https://doi.org/10.1017/9781009019460

Bennett, J. M. (2013). Intercultural competence: Vital perspectives for diversity and inclusion. In Bernardo M. Ferdman & Barbara R. Deane (Eds), *Diversity at work: The practice of inclusion* (pp. 155–176). Wiley. https://doi.org/10.1002/9781118764282.ch5

Council of Europe. (2020). *The Common European Framework of Reference for Languages (CEFR)*. www.coe.int/en/web/common-european-framework-reference-languages

Eddy, J. (2022). *Designing world language curriculum for intercultural communicative competence*. Bloomsbury Academic.

Egitim, S., & Umemiya, Y. (2023). *Leaderful classroom pedagogy through an interdisciplinary lens: Merging theory with practice*. Springer Nature. https://doi.org/10.1007/978-981-99-6655-4

Fantini, A. E. (2018). *Intercultural communicative competence in educational exchange: A multinational perspective*. Routledge. https://doi.org/10.4324/9781351251747

Hajar, A. (2020). Arab sojourner expectations, academic socialization, and strategy use in a pre-sessional English programme in Britain. *Pedagogies: An International Journal, 15*(3), 221–239. https://doi.org/10.1080/1554480X.2019.1696200

Harumi, S. (1999). The use of silence by Japanese learners of English in cross-cultural communication and its pedagogical implications. [Unpublished doctoral thesis], UCL Institute of Education, UK

Harumi, S. (2011). Classroom silence: Voices from Japanese EFL learners. *ELT Journal*, *65*(3), 260–269. https://doi.org/10.1093/elt/ccq046

Harumi, S. (2020). Approaches to interacting with classroom silence: The role of teacher talk. In J. King & S. Harumi (Eds.), *East Asian perspectives on silence in English language education* (pp. 37–59). Multilingual Matters. https://doi.org/10.21832/9781788926775-008

Harumi, S. (2023a). Classroom silence and learner-initiated repair: Using conversation analysis-informed material design to develop interactional repertoires. *TESOL Journal*, *14*(1), 1–18. https://doi.org/10.1002/tesj.704

Harumi, S. (2023b). The mediative role of learning materials: Raising L2 learners' awareness of silence and conversational repair during L2 interaction. *Journal of Silence Studies in Education*, *2*(2), 145–162. https://doi.org/10.31763/jsse.v2i2.79

Harumi, S. (2024). Multiple-contextual perspectives on silence: A narrative case study. *Neofilolog*, *63*(2) 265–292. https://doi.org/10.14746/n.2024.63.2.3

Holliday, A., Hyde, A., & Kullman, J. (2021). *Intercultural communication: An advanced resource book for students* (4th ed.). Routledge. https://doi.org/10.4324/9780367482480

Hooper, D., Egitim, S., & Hofhuis, J. (2025). Exploring the impact of near-peer role modeling on learners' basic psychological needs: Insights from English Classes in Japanese Higher Education. *International Journal of Educational Research Open*, *8*(1), 1–12. https://doi.org/10.1016/j.ijedro.2024.100429

Hooper, D. (2025). Mediating educational transitions with near-peer role models in the language classroom. *TESL-EJ, 28*(4), 1–19. https://doi.org/10.55593/ej.28112a6

King, J. (2013). *Silence in the second language classroom*. Springer Nature. https://doi.org/10.1057/9781137301482

Kireeti, K., Egitim, S., & Thomson, B. J. (2024). Utilizing peer evaluation as a collaborative learning tool: Fostering autonomy satisfaction in English presentation classes. *Language Learning in Higher Education*, *14*(2), 379–400. https://doi.org/10.1515/cercles-2024-0037

Kogure, M. (2007). Nodding and smiling in silence during the loop sequence of backchannels in Japanese conversation. *Journal of Pragmatics*, *39*(7), 1275–1289. https://doi.org/10.1016/j.pragma.2007.02.011

Kramsch, C. (1998). *Language and Culture*. Oxford University Press.

Maynard, S. (1989). *Japanese conversation: Self-contextualization through structure and interactional management*. Ablex.

McConachy, T., & Liddicoat, A. J. (2022). Introduction: Second language pragmatics for intercultural understanding. In T. McConachy & A. J. Liddicoat (Eds.), *Teaching and learning second language pragmatics for intercultural understanding* (pp. 1–18). Routledge. https://doi.org/10.4324/9781003094128

Richards, K. (2006). "Being the teacher": Identity and classroom observation. *Applied Linguistics*, 27: 51–77. https://doi.org/10.1093/applin/ami041

Sábcgez-Hernández, A., & Maíz-Arévalo, C. (2022). Toward a new measurement of intercultural competence: Assessing the pragmatic competence of intercultural speakers. In T. McConachy & A. J. Liddicoat (Eds.), *Teaching and learning second language pragmatics for intercultural understanding* (pp. 119–226). Routledge. https://doi.org/10.4324/9781003094128

Spencer-Oatey, H., Franklin, P., & Lazidou, D. (2022). *Global fitness for global people: How to manage and leverage cultural diversity at work*. Castledown. https://doi.org/10.29140/9780648184430

Thomas, J. (1983). Cross-cultural pragmatic failure. *Applied Linguistics*, *4*(2), 91–112. https://doi.org/10.1093/applin/4.2.91

6

Pedagogical Insights for Enhancing Global Competence in the Classroom and Beyond

Seiko Harumi and Soyhan Egitim

6.1 East Asian Learners' Study Abroad Experiences and Tandem Learning

Since 2019, the learning environment for L2 learners has dramatically changed due to the COVID-19 pandemic and technological advances, notably the use of online communication tools. These changes have provided invaluable opportunities for L2 learners to communicate more easily with first language (L1) speakers of their target language via online communication and various digital applications. Moreover, the number of opportunities for study abroad has been gradually increasing since the end of the pandemic. However, Kariya (2024) warns that Japanese students' study abroad peaked in the early 2000s, and there is a continuing inward-looking tendency. As outlined in Chapter 1, there are significant gaps between governmental policies aimed at enhancing intercultural opportunities and the educational contexts required for their implementation. As a first step in appraising these opportunities, this section explores the benefits of study abroad and tandem learning, including language exchanges and Collaborative Online International Learning (COIL), by reviewing findings from recent investigations into pedagogical activities involving East Asian learners.

In recent years, opportunities for study abroad have highlighted the role of diverse regional contexts. While East Asian learners' favorite destinations for study abroad remain the so-called inner circle countries (Kachru, 1986) such as the United States, Australia, Canada, and Britain (Halenko & Economidou-Kogetsidis, 2022; Humphries et al., 2023), where English is considered the native language, there has been a notable increase in the popularity of study abroad opportunities in outer circle locations where English as a Lingua Franca (ELF) (Kobayashi, 2018) is widely used. These contexts include the Philippines (Ikeda, 2020), Malaysia, Finland (Kelly & Imamura, 2024; Nam, 2018), Sweden (Siegel, 2022), and Thailand (Fukada, 2017; Kimura, 2019). These destinations offer practical benefits for sojourners, including lower financial outlay and less stringent target language proficiency requirements. They can also be attractive due to a diminished affective filter, with students feeling less anxious about interacting with target-language speakers who are not L1-native speakers (Humphries et al., 2023; Kobayashi, 2018; Umino, 2023). This may also lead to a heightened awareness of the pragmatic role of English as a communication tool. The effectiveness of study abroad in individual contexts depends on the type of program (e.g., short-term, year-long exchange, academic English, EMI, or degree programs). Recent studies have explored the benefits and challenges of these destinations. We will examine these findings from the perspective of intercultural L2 interaction.

The overall effects of studying abroad have often been explored through quantitative research. For example, Warchulski and Ward (2022) surveyed the effects of over six months of study abroad on 935 Japanese learners of English language. The results indicated that students positively engage with English even outside the classroom, adopting positive and proactive approaches to intercultural communication. Similarly, Burden's (2020) large-scale quantitative study found that study abroad contexts provide an environment that enables learners to transform from anxious learners of English, governed by negative self-perception, to L2 users with more positive outlooks, aware of the need to use English as a communicative tool. Furthermore, Kelly and Imamura's qualitative interview study (2024) in Finland, which explored Japanese English language learners' self-belief in their use of multiple languages and perceptions towards English language learning, reported similar findings. These studies suggested that English language learning in Japan is predominantly examination-oriented, whereas in Finland, students found themselves using English as a communicative tool. Erduyan and Bazar's study (2022) of Japanese learners of Turkish who participated in a study abroad in Turkey produced similar findings. These learners had negative perceptions of themselves as English language learners, which made it difficult for them to be positive about studying English in Japan. This was in stark contrast to their learning experience when they studied Turkish in Turkey, where they enjoyed their sojourn. These studies illustrate Japanese learners' awareness of the role of English as an interactional resource and the positive effects of study abroad, as well as the opportunities it provides for learners to reflect on the way they use English as a world language (EWL) education context in Japan.

Furthermore, Ikeda's study (2020) shows how 14 Japanese students studying in the Philippines became aware of the need to answer questions in conversation, an interactional competence required to clarify their understanding. These students seemed to easily acquire useful interactional resources such as fillers and formulaic expressions, including "oh, yeah" and "that's what I mean," to maintain conversation. On the other hand, Siegel's (2022) study on Japanese short-term exchange students attending English-medium instruction (EMI) programs in Sweden at the university level indicated that it was difficult for them to participate in class, despite their EMI class experiences in Japan. The challenges included: (1) the fast speech of Swedish or German students who were more proficient in English, (2) unfamiliar conversational turn-taking systems, which required Japanese students to initiate or intervene, and (3) a lack of background and subject knowledge. While they partially overcame these difficulties through preparation in advance or peer support, Siegel's study (2022) suggests that it is important for teachers to be aware of these difficulties and provide appropriate support before and during the sojourn. Furthermore, both the autoethnographic study by Fukada (2017) in the United States and the study by Kimura (2019) exploring the role of ELF for Japanese exchange students studying abroad in Thailand suggested that affinity spaces such as sports had positive roles for the participants, helping them engage in intercultural communication by sharing common interests.

In the case of the role of third languages, Nam's study (2018) on a Korean exchange student in Finland illustrated the limitations on students' ability to communicate in English in non-English speaking contexts due to the additional requirement to learn Finnish. On the other hand, Kimura's study (2019) reported the positive role that the Thai language played in fostering rapport among local and Japanese students through shared interests such as pop culture. These empirical studies reveal both positive and challenging aspects of study abroad, highlighting the importance of: (1) raising L2 learners' awareness of the nature of intercultural interaction in L2, (2) setting expectations when using L2 as an interactional tool, (3) understanding learners' facilitative and inhibitive encounters within intercultural contexts, and (4) providing pedagogical support. They also emphasize the crucial role of enhancing learners' cross-cultural knowledge and fostering flexibility to adopt new communicative styles beyond their horizons (Egitim, 2022, 2023).

Turning to e-tandem learning, there has been a dramatic increase in the number of programs of this type, and empirical studies report its effects as a new approach to enhancing intercultural interaction across continents. Notable examples include programs involving Japanese learners of the English language (Akiyama, 2017; Hamada & Iwasaki, 2024; Ikeda, 2020; Nishino & Nakatsugawa, 2020; Sabban-Taylor, 2021). A recent large-scale quantitative study by Hamada and Iwasaki (2024) examined the effects of a one-on-one tele-tandem language exchange program between Australian university students learning Japanese and Japanese learners of English language at a Japanese university. Learners' self-reports throughout the survey indicated positive overall effects, such as increased behavioral engagement, higher communication frequency in L2, and enhanced emotional engagement. These factors collectively improved their willingness to communicate in the target language to build interpersonal relationships. Learners' initiation often involved the use of digital media, such as YouTube, video games, Instagram, and even online *Shogi* (Japanese chess), which helped reduce awkward silences during exchanges. The study highlighted that learner-initiated language activities play a critical role in enhancing intercultural communication. Such activities not only fostered more inclusive cultural sensitivities but also demonstrated the potential of online communication to promote diverse, meaningful interactions. However, certain limitations remain, including the absence of spontaneous non-verbal cues and challenges in systematically integrating online activities into traditional curricula.

In the case of qualitative studies involving the pragmatic use of L2 in intercultural communication through tele-tandem L2 learning, the concept of shared belief system (Brace & Newman, 1978, cited in Varonis & Gass, 1985, p. 336) is a useful analytical lens. It reveals ways in which intercultural communication can be both challenging and rewarding because certain differences and the lack of shared schematic knowledge in mutual belief systems can have unintended consequences or lead to misunderstandings. For example, Varonis and Gass (1985) reported this type of interactional difficulty in telephone conversations between native and non-native speakers of English, with both participants lapsing into silence with puzzled expressions on their faces.

Further, Nishino and Nakatsugawa (2020) observe that these miscommunications can arise from differences in communicative styles and their underlying values, such as (1) length of communication within a turn, (2) prioritization of relevance, (3) social conventions, and (4) response time. In their study, which explores the use of text messaging as a medium for tele-tandem learning exchange between American and Japanese university students communicating in English and Japanese, they refer to an American student who is perplexed when he receives text message replies much sooner than expected and, in turn, tries to respond more frequently himself. He is also concerned about his Japanese learning partner's passive reticence in topic development and questioning. At the same time, the Japanese participant finds it difficult to determine the right moments to ask questions, although she is aware of differences in culturally oriented communicative values and frequency of questions. Similarly, Akiyama's (2017) study on telecollaboration between American and Japanese students highlights that differing expectations around waiting time can hinder the smooth flow of conversations unless both parties collaborate to adjust their communication timing styles. Examining turn length, Carnals's (2024) study on e-tandem virtual exchanges between Spanish and English students found that Spanish speakers' lengthy monologues led one English student to abandon attempts at asking questions.

As recent studies on study abroad programs and e-tandem learning suggest, these educational activities are highly beneficial, offering authentic opportunities for learners to interact, driven by genuine motivation. These opportunities for intercultural communication play a critical role in fostering learning through differences. However, virtual exchange programs, such as e-tandem learning or COIL, come with their fair share of challenges. Since students often come from diverse cultural and linguistic backgrounds, differences in linguistic proficiency, communication styles, non-verbal cues, and cultural nuances can lead to imbalanced participation. In this context, teachers play a crucial role as facilitators. To manage these cross-cultural interactions effectively, it is more important than ever for EWL teachers to have a sufficient understanding of these nuances and differences (Egitim, 2024a). While much of the research focuses on students' intercultural competence or the general role of language in intercultural communication (Byram, 1997, 2009; Deardorff, 2006; Fantini, 2018), there has been relatively less attention paid to how language teachers themselves develop and apply intercultural competence in their teaching practice (Egitim, 2024). As *global competence* gains increasing significance in world language education (used instead of foreign language education), the role of teachers as facilitators—both through the languages they teach and through their approach to communication, teaching methods, and cultural awareness—cannot be overstated.

Furthermore, studies have linked world language teachers' (WLTs) intercultural competence with students' oral participation in both Japan and China (Chen et al., 2014; Egitim, 2024b). The findings from a mixed-methods study by Egitim (2024a) show that WLTs' proficiency in the host language and understanding of the host culture are positively correlated with increased student oral participation. The study also emphasizes the importance of WLTs demonstrating intercultural competence by incorporating group work, tolerating silence, and sharing personal anecdotes and cultural stories to create a psychologically safe environment that encourages student expression. Another study conducted by Chen et al. (2014) on cross-cultural adaptation of WLTs in China suggests that teachers' intercultural competence and proficiency in the local language significantly affect their ability to interact with students and foster greater engagement in the classroom. The study highlighted how teachers' adaptation to cultural and linguistic differences could influence students' willingness to participate, especially in world language classes.

While no studies have focused on language teachers' intercultural competence in facilitating tele-tandem learning for students from diverse cultural backgrounds, this chapter aims to serve as a starting point by offering practical suggestions to help teachers support students in navigating the challenges posed by virtual exchange programs.

One effective means of preventing imbalanced participation in online platforms is to set clear guidelines for turn-taking from the outset. By explaining how conversations should flow—such as encouraging equal speaking time and promoting active listening—teachers help students understand the importance of balanced participation. Furthermore, in virtual exchanges, teachers can observe the flow of conversation and step in if imbalances occur. For instance, the teacher, observing the conversation, notices that *Emily* (an American student) is speaking continuously, and *Haruto* (a Japanese student) seems hesitant to contribute. The teacher decides to intervene gently to restore balance: The teacher (in the chat or verbally) says, "Emily, you've shared some great insights about work-life balance in the U.S. I'd like to hear Haruto's thoughts on this topic as well. Haruto, what is work-life balance like in Japan? Do you agree with some of the points that Emily mentioned?" By intervening in this way, the interculturally competent teacher ensures both students have the opportunity to express themselves while also guiding the conversation to foster further interaction between them.

Teachers can emphasize the importance of active listening, which involves not just waiting for a turn to speak but genuinely engaging with the other person's words. We emphasize this point in the third component of our framework, *adaptability in communication styles* as well. Encouraging feedback from both parties, where students summarize or comment on what the other has said, ensures that both participants stay involved and valued in the conversation (Kireeti et al., 2024). This leads us to reflective practice, which helps students become more aware of how they contribute to the conversation and learn how to adjust their behavior in future virtual intercultural encounters (Mann & Walsh, 2017). Below is a demonstration of how reflective practice can be applied in a tele-tandem context.

The teacher invites the students to engage in reflective practice:

> *Let's take a moment to reflect on the conversation. How did you feel during the exchange? Were there moments when you felt you were able to share your ideas comfortably, or were there challenges in getting your point across?*

Emily's Reflection:

I realized that I talked quite a lot during the discussion. I didn't give Haruto much space to share his thoughts. I should have asked him more questions and made sure to listen more actively.

Haruto's Reflection:

I felt a bit hesitant to speak because Emily was sharing so much. It was hard for me to jump in. Next time, I'll try to be more assertive and share my views even if I'm unsure.

As illustrated in the example above, incorporating reflective practice provides students with the opportunity to gain a deeper understanding of their role in conversations and helps them adjust their behavior for more balanced and effective participation. Especially, in virtual intercultural contexts, where the lack of non-verbal cues and the challenges of managing turn-taking can complicate communication, reflective practice—facilitated by the teacher—helps students grow as communicators and become better equipped to handle the challenges of online intercultural encounters.

6.2 Practical Applications of *Global Competence* Development

In this section, we introduce pedagogical practices designed to promote intercultural communication through tandem learning. One of the authors, Seiko, shares two examples. The first, visitor sessions, is an activity integrated into the Japanese language program of a year-long intensive beginner course at a UK university, involving native Japanese speakers participating in online classroom activities. The second is a collaborative, extracurricular, eight-week tele-tandem language exchange program for English and Japanese university students. We hope these practices, which utilize our Four-Step Framework for developing *global competence*, provide valuable insights for teachers interested in implementing similar methods and offer fresh perspectives on current pedagogical practices.

6.2.1 Intercultural Interaction Between Japanese English Language Learners and Japanese Language Learners in the UK

Through the visitor session activity, Seiko provides Japanese language learners with authentic opportunities to engage in intercultural communication with native Japanese speakers. The practice, adaptable to other languages and educational contexts, integrates seamlessly into a year-long curriculum and serves as a model for combining language learning with cultural immersion, even in online environments. Below, Seiko outlines the context, methodology, and evolution of this activity, emphasizing its role in supporting beginner-level students in achieving CEFR A2 proficiency.

6.2.1.1 Visitor Sessions: Face-to-Face vs. Online

First, Seiko shares the pedagogical practices she has adopted in Japanese language classrooms for students studying for degree courses in the UK. Although the target language in this practice is Japanese, this activity can be adapted for the study of any language by following the basic elementary-level procedure explained below or by making modifications. This is an ongoing pedagogical practice incorporated into a year-long elementary-level Japanese language curriculum over several years. Seiko first explains the context and how this language activity has been incorporated into the curriculum. However, this activity can be adapted to suit different contact hours, pedagogical circumstances, and needs in individual educational contexts with modifications. She then introduces current practices in her course as an example.

With eight weekly contact hours in a year-long degree program, Seiko's intensive Japanese language module aims to bring students to the CEFR A2 level by the end of the year. Students' prior Japanese language learning experiences vary, ranging from complete beginners to those who have studied for General Certificate of Secondary Education (GCSE), A-levels, or the International Baccalaureate (IB), as well as self-taught learners. However, based on a placement test conducted at the start of the academic year, all students are assigned to this elementary-level course and divided into one of three groups according to their prior knowledge of Japanese.

The pedagogical practice called the visitor session was implemented in the aforementioned elementary-level speaking class long before the current online practice was widely adopted during the pandemic. The original motive for this language activity was to give L2 learners opportunities to interact with L1 Japanese speakers in natural contexts during their first encounters. This allowed them to use the target language to improve their confidence in speaking, try out the language they had acquired in the classroom, and immerse themselves in exchanges with Japanese visitors, exposing them to cultural aspects of the Japanese language. Visitors interested in this activity, who are volunteers, were initially invited to visit classrooms in person twice a year, in the tenth week of Terms 1 and 2. They come from various backgrounds, including international students, international exchange students, academics, stay-at-home spouses, professionals such as translators, writers, teachers of languages other than Japanese, charity workers, and advanced learners of Japanese (senior students).

Although this practice transitioned online during and after the pandemic, its key principle remained unchanged. The primary purpose of these sessions, aligned with the curriculum outlined above, was to provide all L2 learners in the module with authentic opportunities to engage in intercultural communication. In recent years, previous studies suggested that L2 learners have had various informal opportunities to participate in such interactions outside classroom hours, including (1) conversation-for-learning activities (Kasper & Kim, 2015), (2) numerous language exchange or conversation clubs/cafes (Bao, 2019) that foster L2 social communicative skills, (3) language or culture-related societies, and (4) locally organized campus meetings. However, Seiko's visitor sessions are designed to offer these opportunities to all students enrolled in the language module, starting from the beginner level, as an integral part of the program.

6.2.1.2 Pedagogical Framework

The pedagogical framework adopted in Seiko's visitor sessions, as described above, is an adaptation of the Four-Step Framework for cultivating *global competence* proposed in this book. Table 6.1 outlines the specific components integrated into these four steps. In Step 1, which focuses on building world language proficiency (used instead of foreign language), one of the main challenges is aligning the session's timescale within a university program. This involves a minimum of 80 contact hours over ten weeks, aiming for an achievement level close to A1. This foundation equips students with the confidence and readiness to use the target language effectively.

Step 2 introduces cross-cultural knowledge through dedicated sessions on interactional strategies such as fillers, repair mechanisms, and Japanese listenership while comparing them to their English equivalents. This helps learners become more aware of how to utilize these conversational tools naturally. Step 3 emphasizes authentic intercultural experiences, where both learners and L1 speakers are encouraged to maintain conversations using any available resources, including gestures, drawings, online chat, physical objects, images, and translanguaging when necessary. Finally, Step 4 employs reflection sheets to enhance learners' awareness of their language use, communication styles, and new insights, while also setting goals for further improvement. Similar sessions, adapted for Japanese contexts of EWL, are discussed in another study (Harumi, 2023a), which includes a needs analysis of English language learners (see Table 6.1).

6.2.1.3 Practical Procedure

The participants are a class teacher (Seiko), students (up to twenty per group), and visitors. Visitors are recruited through internal college emails inviting advanced learners and exchange students, and also externally through Seiko's network of colleagues working with learners of English language education in Japan and elsewhere. Visitors are informed about the aim of the session, learners' language proficiency level, and the types of questions and topics used to start conversations.

TABLE 6.1 *Four-Step Framework for Global Competence: Visitor Session for Intercultural Interaction (VSIC)*

Step 1 World language proficiency	Step 2 Cross-cultural knowledge	Step 3 Adaptability in communication styles	Step 4 Values beyond horizon
Classroom practice Preparation for visitor sessions	Introduction to interactional resources: (e.g., Japanese listenership, *aizuchi* and comparison to English non-verbal communication, use of repair, formal vs informal speech styles)	Intercultural interaction with L1-speaking visitors	Raising awareness of diverse cultural values through reflection and preparation for next session: (e.g., Listenership in Japanese, variations in *aizuchi*, topic-development, repair, speech style)

Step 1:
To prepare for the visitor sessions, learners need to ensure they can introduce themselves, refer to their basic backgrounds, speak about their likes and dislikes using basic adjectives, and talk about their basic daily routines using different tenses and adverbs required to elicit answers from visitors.

Step 2:
Learners need to harness interactional resources such as listenership in Japanese and the use of repair using fillers or questions, which are taught in Term 1. Additionally, one week before the visitor session, learners are given a set of questions and topics to start conversations with visitors. These questions are reviewed together in class. Visitors receive the same information, along with learners' background details. Both parties are encouraged to prepare possible topics for discussion in the session after reviewing the provided questions and topics, which they may choose to supplement.

Step 3:
The one-hour session begins with a five-minute introduction, during which all participants briefly introduce themselves. The introduction of online visitor sessions has enabled the inclusion of visitors from various countries and regions, such as Hawaii, Finland, Holland, and different parts of Japan. Sessions often begin with an icebreaker question, such as asking where participants are located or what they ate for breakfast, lunch, or dinner. This is followed by a ten-minute practice session (see PowerPoint slides for examples of questions and topics used in practice: see images 1–3), where students review topics to discuss in breakout rooms with the visitors, often using images as prompts. Afterward, participants are divided into breakout rooms.

The ratio of students to visitors varies depending on attendance that day. To account for potential technical issues on both sides, the teacher, acting as a moderator, must remain flexible when forming groups. Typically, a ratio of one visitor to two students works well, as it helps reduce psychological pressure for both parties. Next, there are two or three group rotations, with each breakout session lasting approximately 15 minutes. This structure gives students opportunities to speak with different visitors during the one-hour session. While participants initially use prepared questions for the first few minutes, the goal is to engage in spontaneous conversation for the remaining 10 minutes. The session concludes with either students asking visitors about their backgrounds or sharing the visitors' recommendations on Japan and related topics.

In recent years, Seiko has also invited Japanese learners of the English language to speak about their university in Japan or study abroad experiences as additional elements within this session. As her students study abroad in their third year, they are motivated to listen to these presentations and learn about life in Japanese universities. One Japanese student, who spoke about her life as a university student in Tokyo and her study abroad experiences in Finland during this visitor session, pointed out differences in educational environments (see images 4 and 5). A student from Kansai talked about the differences between lifestyles in Tokyo and Kansai, including the cost of living. Another student from

Tokyo spoke about her study abroad experience in China, along with her university life in Tokyo and the unique characteristics of her university. Images from the first ten-minute practice stage, extracted from a PowerPoint document, can be seen below (see images 1–3). These samples illustrate the intended basic use of vocabulary and grammar in the first session. The main purpose of this initial session is for learners to use their knowledge and skills in their first encounters with visitors so that they can experience real communication, which requires spontaneous interaction or improvisation according to the predetermined context, and also to start conversations (see Figure 6.1).

Step 4:
Learners reflect on their use of the target language by completing a reflection sheet involving task completion. For example, in the very first session, they reflect on their task achievement, focusing on self-introduction, comprehension of visitors' backgrounds, general understanding of key information exchanged, maintenance of conversation, and use of pauses or fillers. They also provide self-reflective comments when completing these statements, starting with the formats: (1) I think I was particularly good at …, (2) I found that it was difficult to …, or (3) I would like to improve…. This final reflection serves to raise awareness of learners' use of the target language and encourages them to observe other interactional styles and set targets to achieve for the next session. In the following section, voices from Japanese language learners, English language learners, and visitors share their experiences to highlight the benefits and challenges of these visitor sessions, seen as examples of intercultural communication.

6.2.2 Lessons in Intercultural Communication: Perspectives from Multiple Voices

In this section, Seiko shares the voices of L2 learners and visitors, along with her own, articulating the benefits of these visitor sessions, which connect learners with people outside the classroom by using their target language. We look at facilitative dimensions as a form of intercultural education, using multiple perspectives, which help us see the overall picture.

Please ask Q1-5 by taking turns. (13分)

Q1 Ask her・his name

おなまえはなんですか。

Q2 What do you do? What is your job?

おしごとはなんですか。

Q3(a) Where are you studying?

どこでべんきょうしていますか。

What are you studying?

なにをべんきょうしていますか。

Q3(b) Where are you working?

どこではたらいていますか。

Q4 How is your study (or job)?

おしごと / べんきょうはどうですか。

Q5 Where are you living in?

どこにすんでいますか。

FIGURE 6.1 *Key Questions for Practice Before Entering Break-out Rooms*
Image 1. Initial Topics Image 2. Questions on Japan Image 3. Further questions

6.2.2.1 Learners of Japanese as a World Language

As mentioned earlier, each class consists of 15–20 students and 7–8 visitors. Most visitors participate in a single one-hour session, though some stay for two or three sessions. The following comments are from two students who attended both sessions in Terms 1 and 2, held 12 weeks apart. This interval allows learners to observe their progress in speaking skills over time. In this section, Seiko highlights the experiences of two students to trace their development between the two sessions.

First session, week 10, Term 1 (after 80 contact hours)
In this first session, students began with self-introductions, also asking and answering questions to exchange basic personal information. Students completed reflection sheets referred to in Step 4 above, highlighting their observations on satisfactory or challenging aspects of their interaction during the session.

ここは日本のどこですか？
何をしますか？

A. 花火（はなび）
B. 花見（はなみ）
C. かぶき
D. ゆきまつり

Q1: 先生はどこから来ましたか。
A1:: ながさきから来ました。

Q2: ながさきは　なに　が　おいしいですか。

A2: カステラ　が　おいしいです。

Q3: （ながさきは）なに　が　ゆうめいですか。

ちゃんぽんがゆうめいです。

Any other questions about Nagasaki?

FIGURE 6.1 (Continued)

Students' reflections on fulfilling experiences:

The first student noted that her confidence in using the language, her emotional state, and her comprehension were strong during the session. She further highlighted that the rotation of discussions with different visitors significantly boosted her confidence:

> I think that I used various grammar points. I believe that I was friendly ☺. I didn't find it difficult to understand the visitors. In the second breakout room, I found it easier to be more open, ask more questions, and answer with longer sentences. (Student A)

The other student emphasized his confidence in listenership skills, highlighting other aspects of interaction, including spontaneous turn-taking, clarification requests, and comprehension:

> I think I was good at using fillers and Aizuchi [back-channeling cues such as nodding]. For the most part, I think I was also able to understand fairly well and could ask for the speaker to repeat themselves/clarify their meaning if I misunderstood. I was able to ask spontaneous questions I hadn't thought of beforehand and understand the responses I received. (Student B)

These students also mentioned the following challenges they encountered.

Students' reflections on challenging experiences:
Student A mentioned that she found it difficult to expand conversations, particularly when it came to the spontaneous use of questions. She emphasized the importance of practice and noted that she found the second rotation easier to handle. However, she is also acutely aware of her misuse of grammar during the session and recalls specific instances of it:

> It was difficult to extend the conversation and ask very specific questions on the spot. I thought of them a bit later. In the second breakout room, it was a bit easier as we had practiced, but I was still a bit nervous. I am sorry, I said 'o dekimasu (can do xxx-incorrect object marker, 'o' is used)' instead of 'ga' (correct use of particle indicating the object of the action)' when I was summarizing our conversation with a Visitor. (Student A)

Student B also commented on the difficulties of maintaining a conversation, particularly when dealing with silence, and expressed concerns about politeness in his use of language:

> *I often had long unnatural pauses in my speech when trying to answer questions on the spot. I often did not stick to a polite or plain style consistently – I would often trail off or not end sentences properly or would add the incorrect sentence ending when I realized my omission. (Student B)*

The second student's self-reflection also illustrates certain aspects of language use, such as speech style (informal vs. formal), which is unique in Japanese. However, this student also finds it difficult to maintain a conversation while dealing with silence when answering questions. These comments indicate that back-channeling cues and reactive tokens (*Aizuchi*) can be used effectively at fairly early stages, but the skills needed to manage and maintain conversation are highly challenging. Topic development and the use of silence in question-and-answer sequences are particularly problematic. This mirrors the findings of Seiko Harumi's study (2023b). The same student (Student B) had both satisfactory and challenging experiences with the use of silence within interactional flow, highlighting the demands of conversational flow.

Second session: week 10, Term 2 (after 160 contact hours)
In the second session, students began with self-introductions, asking and answering questions. The main task for learners in this session was to ask the visitors for recommendations (e.g., places to visit, things to do) in preparation for their upcoming study abroad experience in Japan. After the questions and visitors' responses, the session continued with free conversation.

Students' reflections on fulfilling experiences:
The first student noted that she improved her ability to use a wider range of expressions for further explanation or elaboration

and even enjoyed maintaining the conversational flow with increased confidence. The student elaborated further:

> *This time I used more grammar, and I was able to explain things when I was asked to elaborate. I asked questions and found it very fun to keep the conversation flowing, I think I was more confident in the first breakout room. I think I was good at introducing myself and answering questions about myself as well as asking the visitors. (Student A).*

The second student also elaborated on his positive experience of maintaining the conversational flow:

> *I was able to have good conversations with both of the groups I participated in. I was able to express myself well, understand and respond to the conversation partners, and ask them to repeat themselves when I didn't understand. I think I used Aizuchi well mostly. I think I was better at continuing the conversation or asking for more information when one of us finished responding to the other. I think I was able to be more confident and could answer faster and more naturally to basic questions. (Student B).*

This student specifically referred to his improved ability to ask follow-up questions.

Students' reflections on fulfilling experiences:
However, both students reflected on matters they would like to improve further:

> *I found it difficult to elaborate when asked about the story of anime. In the second breakout room I was a bit less confident, I found it a bit more difficult to keep the conversation in the second room. I forgot to use many fillers- I did use them a few times, but I had chances to use them more. One weak point during the second session that I remember is that I wasn't able to elaborate enough when I was asked about the plot of an*

> *anime. While I was able to give the basic structure of it, I didn't explain some details. Because I was in a breakout room with only one other participant, I found it difficult to talk all the time and keep the conversation going. (Student A)*

In her self-reflection, Student A mentions that she struggled to elaborate on a topic, feeling that she didn't perform as well, partly because it was difficult to explain certain details and also because of the number of participants in the breakout room. This point is discussed in the following section which deals with further considerations.

> *There were a few moments when I couldn't figure out how to express something and ended up saying something simpler, which wasn't exactly what I meant. I'm sure this will improve as I continue studying. Sometimes, I also forgot to add 'ka' (the question marker) to my questions, which made them sound like statements and probably confused people." (Student B)*

Student B mentions limitations in the use of certain expressions. He opts for simpler expressions and sometimes uses question markers. He nevertheless appears to be more objectively analyzing the way he uses a range of expressions. These two students' reflections on the two sessions illustrate improved and challenging aspects of interaction and the way they focus on their use of language. Nevertheless, their voices reflect the essential nature of authentic interaction for people talking in the target language in their first encounters.

Japanese-speaking visitor's reflection:

Nana, a Japanese exchange student, joined a visitor session from Finland, where she was studying for one year. Nana reflected on her experiences:

> *I joined this visitor session as a visitor and a presenter while I was studying abroad in Finland (Figure 6.2), as my teacher in Japan shared this information about this online session. As I had the experience of helping international students at my*

home university in Japan, I had been wondering if I could do something similar while studying abroad. When I was helping advanced learners of Japanese at my university back in Japan, I was more likely to support them by explaining how to use unfamiliar vocabulary while I was conversing with them. However, students in the visitor session had just started learning Japanese, so I myself learned how to teach or guide them through conversation. Although the proficiency level differed according to the individual, I felt their speaking skills were improving as they were not hesitant to speak and kept on persevering. As this session was online, I was able to converse with different people in groups, listen to others with diverse perspectives, and make discoveries, both as a speaker and as a listener. I was impressed with the students' broad knowledge of Japanese food, which may be down to many Japanese restaurants in London. I felt this session really helped to motivate students to learn Japanese in the UK, giving them ready access to Japanese speakers, such as me, having joined this session online while in Finland.

(Nana, a Japanese student studying English abroad in Finland, translated by the author)

Another Japanese exchange student, who studied in Belgium, joined a face-to-face visitor session while visiting the UK after two months of a year-long study abroad programme and shared her experiences.

I participated in this visitor session at a UK university because I believed that the experience of communicating with learners of Japanese would enrich my life. My specific reasons for participating included exploring a European city I had never visited before, giving a presentation to Japanese language students, and communicating with them in their own language. I was also interested in learning about their positive attitudes toward learning Japanese, which they had started after entering university, as well as their enthusiasm for communicating in Japanese. By joining the session and observing their positive attitude while trying to communicate in Japanese—despite occasional mistakes in grammar or vocabulary—I realized that I, too, should make an effort to communicate in English, even if I make mistakes, just as they did. I found this type of session to be highly beneficial for students learning second languages. Such opportunities enrich practical language use, foster cultural awareness, and, in turn, enhance motivation to continue learning a second language (Misuzu, an exchange student in Belgium).

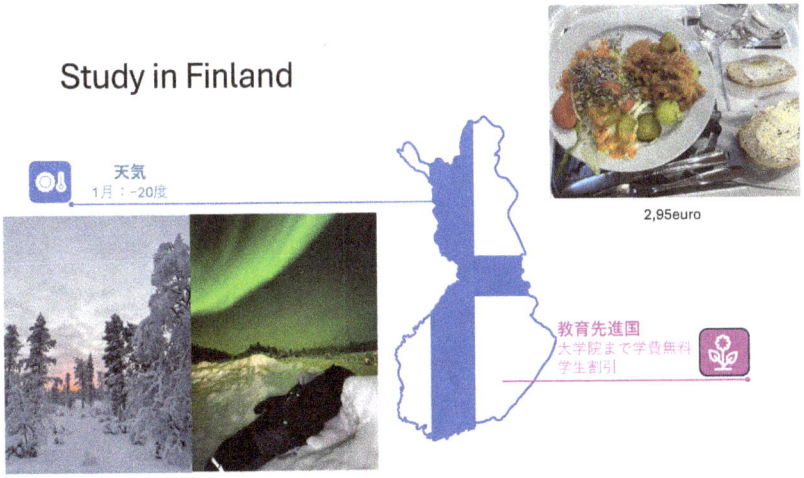

FIGURE 6.2 *Nana's Study Abroad Presentation Slides*
Image 4. Studying in Finland Image 5. Learning environments

Another Japanese exchange student who was in her sixth month of study abroad at a UK university shared her experiences.

> My chief motive for joining this session was the desire to communicate with students from diverse backgrounds. When I was at university in Japan, I really enjoyed communicating with international students and that also motivated me. I feel that by talking with students in the UK, I was able to learn about real British life. For example, British students I met recommended British foods I did not learn about when I had searched on my own, and I also discovered many differences between university life in Japan and in the UK. Despite being on a study abroad program, I felt that it is was difficult for me to learn about authentic British lifestyles. So, it was great to learn more about British life and to get closer to British friends. In that sense, to be able to learn real life through this session was great. It is often difficult to understand the reality just by doing academic research or by using your imagination. However, this type of session provided me with valuable experiences during my study abroad, which was something I had aspire to. I was also glad when British students told me how they were able to learn about the real Japan by communicating with me and through my presentation. So, I thought that, for both sides, this session was really motivating and useful (Yumika, an exchange student in the UK).

While Misuzu and Yumika were participating in study abroad programs in different countries—Belgium and the UK—they proactively sought opportunities to communicate with students learning Japanese as a self-initiated discursive practice. Reflecting on their experiences, both expressed being inspired by the attitudes of Japanese learners toward L2 acquisition, which significantly boosted their own motivation. Yumika also mentioned that she was able to exchange a variety of cultural topics through genuine communication, rather than relying solely on research or imagination. Their reflections provide valuable insights into how authentic intercultural communication can mutually support L2 learners, not only from linguistic perspectives but also in terms of interactional, emotional, and intercultural growth.

Furthermore, some visitors have been attending sessions continuously for many years. One such visitor, Ayumi, shared her thoughts about these sessions, initial face-to-face events, and also current ones online, discussing her motives for participating and the benefits. Ayumi elaborated on her perspective:

> *I appreciate the opportunity to join the visitor sessions. Each year, I enjoy meeting new students and find every conversation with them very stimulating. My motivation to attend the sessions is to support young people with unlimited futures. Especially students who study Japanese have the potential to become bridges between their countries and Japan. Their interest not only fosters global relationships and creates business opportunities but also makes Japan more familiar to those around them. I believe that getting to know each other's people and cultures can make people feel closer and more positive towards each other. Since the students live outside Japan, they have few opportunities to speak Japanese with native Japanese speakers in their daily lives. The visitor sessions provide valuable practice opportunities, offering students healthy pressure during the first session and helping them gain confidence for the second. One of the session's strengths is that it's not a "language test" but more like a real conversation. After practicing some sentences, we have more personal conversations, talking about ourselves. When discussing topics they are enthusiastic about, students are more likely to feel a sense of accomplishment and satisfaction from sharing a conversation rather than just seeing it as practicing a language they are studying. Additionally, with Visitors from various generations and backgrounds, students can develop new interests and strengthen their motivation to learn Japanese. I also learn many things from the students. For instance, last year, I spoke with a student about a novel she was passionate about. It was so unique that we talked about a Chinese book in Japanese during a session held by a university in the UK. I found the book interesting, looked it up after the session, and was inspired to start studying Chinese. This*

was the unexpected, delightful result of our cultural exchange. Having been a participant in the sessions since 2019, here are some observations as circumstances have changed: Before the global pandemic, there was more pressure on the students as the visitors were physically present. Because of that, I felt that more students took notes during the sessions. During the pandemic, with less in-person contact, some students became shy around people they didn't know well and often kept their cameras off. One advantage of joining from home, however, was that it made it easier to find common interests or explore new topics based on the backgrounds visible on their screens when their cameras were on. After the pandemic, students seem to appreciate the new environment where they can meet in person and stay close to each other. They often join the session with friends, sharing one camera so they can support each other when someone struggles to speak Japanese. I hope that, even with future changes in circumstances, the visitor sessions continue to be a valuable experience for the students. (Visitor, Ayumi).

Ayumi's comments highlight the facilitative role of visitor sessions, their role to motivate learners, their contribution to students' affective factors toward L2 use, and the invaluable opportunities they provide for natural interaction in informal, non-academic contexts. Her observation about the multiple roles of visitor sessions, as spaces where all participants can exchange knowledge of various cultures, is complemented by her enthusiasm for sharing such moments. Furthermore, her insights illustrate the different benefits of these intercultural exchanges in both face-to-face and online formats.

A Japanese-speaking visitor, who is a Chinese teacher and researcher residing in Japan, made the following comments about a visitor session:

I came to Japan as an international student from China almost 30 years ago and have since remained a Chinese language and culture teacher at a Japanese university. As a researcher, I am strongly interested in online collaborative language learning.

Since I was a visiting scholar at a UK university from 2023 to 2024, when I was invited to attend her online Japanese-speaking class, I was delighted to have the opportunity to experience this new approach to foreign language learning. As a teacher involved in world language instruction, the first thing I noticed when speaking with the students was their excitement and bright, sparkling expressions. In the beginning, they appeared a bit nervous, but also eagerly anticipatory. When we started the conversation, we followed a predetermined script (the theme was 'What is your favorite city?'). However, as time went on, their nervousness began to fade, and the conversation naturally diverged from the script. For example, the male student I spoke with was from a city in southern Europe. He began by asking me, 'What is your favorite city?' I responded, 'My favorite city is [city name]. How about you?' He then shared that he liked his hometown. Since I also like his hometown, I asked, 'What is your hometown like?' This made him very happy, and he eagerly talked about how wonderful his hometown is—the food is very delicious; it only takes us two hours to go to his hometown from London, and it is very cheap if you buy the air tickets online; the weather is better than London, and so on. Since his hometown introduction was unscripted and he made a lot of mistakes with vocabulary and grammar, he didn't let these errors hold him back. He expressed himself freely, and his enthusiasm made the conversation enjoyable. As a result, I understood everything he wanted to convey, and his lively expression showed how much he enjoyed the exchange. When I told him I appreciated all the information he shared and I wanted to visit his hometown in the future, he was even happier, smiling shyly as he said, 'I want to go to Japan very much.' This online speaking class allowed the students to experience authentic Japanese pronunciation and speech, confirming that the Japanese they were learning was indeed practical and usable. Moreover, the students gained confidence from receiving praise from native Japanese speakers. These conversations with speakers of the target language demonstrated that the learners' initial, vague interest in language learning could develop into a deeper interest in the

> *target language society. What once required traveling abroad—contact with native speakers/target language speakers—can now be achieved online, as demonstrated in Japanese speaking class. This approach is a sustainable, global, and environmentally friendly method of language education. It will have a significant impact on the teaching of other languages. (Visitor teacher-researcher, Ming)*

Ming holds a unique position as a Japanese-speaking WLT and researcher who contributed as a visitor. Her remarks convey both her own curiosity and enthusiasm, as well as that of the student participant, when discussing even the simplest of topics, such as their favorite town. Her observations also highlight the student's enjoyment in expressing his opinions despite some misuse of language. Furthermore, her comments emphasize the role of online communication as a sustainable pedagogical tool.

6.2.3 Benefits, Challenges, and Future Possibilities

As seen in the comments shared by students and visitors, including English language learners in Japan, visitor sessions provide multiple benefits for participants. Japanese language learners clearly see the value of natural interactions when they have opportunities to observe and experience multiple aspects of conversation in these genuine communication forums. They learn about the role of fillers, repair, and topic development outside dry classroom contexts. Visitors also emphasize that communication in visitor sessions is natural, benefiting from the facilitative role of online interaction. One visitor, who has been attending sessions since 2019, highlighted not only their invaluable authenticity but also their affective benefits to L2 learners, motivating them to communicate across continents and genuine enjoyment of collaborative conversation. This form of intercultural communication inspires her. Her observations on the use of tandem learning in different formats, whether face-to-face or online, provide a useful appraisal of the different media that can facilitate intercultural communication.

It is important to consider the practical challenges involved in preparing visitor sessions, which require careful planning. When organizing this session as part of the curriculum, Seiko faced three main challenges: (1) determining the number of visitors to recruit, (2) group allocation within breakout rooms on the day of the session, and (3) supporting students as they prepare for the sessions. The first challenge, the recruitment of visitors, usually begins one month prior to a session. Depending on the size of the class, the number of visitors can also be a crucial factor. Based on past experience, an optimal ratio of two or three students per visitor is ideal for minimizing psychological and interactional pressures on both participants, as explained in Student A's comment:

> *One weak point during the second session that I remember is that I wasn't able to elaborate enough when I was asked about the plot of an anime. While I was able to give the basic structure of it, I didn't explain some details. Because I was in a breakout room with only one other participant, I found it difficult to talk all the time and keep the conversation going. Compared to the first visitor session when the breakout sessions had at least three or four participants and a smaller weight of the conversation was on me, the second visitor session was a bit more challenging. (Student A)*

Furthermore, it should be noted that some students and visitors prefer one-on-one interactions for more in-depth conversations. As a teacher, it is important to consider individual students' motivation and cognitive readiness. One-on-one sessions may be feasible if subscriptions and attendance on a given day permit, and if there are no unexpected technical or practical issues. However, the teacher must remain attentive and flexible, ready to adapt to any unforeseen changes or issues. Finally, it is important for students to attend a ten-minute preparation session one week prior, during a typical class, to familiarize themselves with the procedures and necessary preparation for the session. While there are some challenging aspects, authentic interaction provides invaluable opportunities for learners to self-assess their interactional competence, referred to as the ability to maintain conversation in sequence during collaborative talk-in- interaction, set new goals, and track their progress over time.

6.2.4 Language and Culture Exchange Program

The second pedagogical practice implemented is a language and culture exchange program involving ten Japanese language learners at a UK university and ten English language learners at a Japanese university over eight weeks. This pedagogical and research project, named "Telecollaborative 'Buddy Systems' for Language Exchange between Japanese and English" (Harumi & Takahashi, 2025), was designed to provide L2 learners with opportunities to interact in natural settings over an eight-week period. This section will introduce this project as a pedagogical practice aimed at raising learners' interactional and intercultural awareness, following the principles of the Four-Step Framework for enriching *global competence* (Egitim & Umemiya, 2023).

6.2.4.1 Why This Started

Despite three decades of applied linguistics research into L2 learners' development of interactional competence in spoken collaborative interaction in both classroom and out-of-class contexts, facilitative methods for promoting these interactional skills and raising cultural awareness of interactional values in learners' target languages within their home contexts, along with internationalization at home (IaH) (Beela & Jones, 2015) and in multilingual settings, have been underexplored. Lack of confidence in L2 spoken interaction has been a prolonged issue, especially for Japanese learners of English. This also applies to learners of Japanese at the post-elementary level, learning L2 in their home country. A recent study (Aubrey, 2017) suggests that intercultural communication can foster L2 learners' interactional competence and promote turn-taking practices in these contexts. This project aimed to involve such opportunities for both English language and Japanese language learners and also to explore the effects of this program as a facilitative pedagogical practice and a scholarly inquiry for the improvement of pedagogical practice.

6.2.4.2 Pedagogical Framework and Procedure

This project explored the effects of telecollaborative 'buddy systems' for tertiary-level language exchange sessions attended by English language learners in Japan and Japanese language learners in the UK. The participants were L2 learners (Japanese and English, CEFR levels A2-B1), learning the target languages before their study abroad programs. The project aimed to develop L2 learners' interactional competence, which is the ability for learners to engage in collaborative talk-in-interaction (Hall et al., 2011) and intercultural awareness, helping them become confident target language users by engaging in intercultural dialogue. Moreover, the project aimed to raise cultural sensitivity towards cross-culturally invisible turn-taking practices in both languages. Thus, the overall pedagogical framework is aligned with the Four-Step Framework proposed in this book to nurture *global competence* at the post-beginner level, aiming to engage in dual language interactions and facilitate a wider interactional and intercultural scope beyond learners' own horizons. The learners participated in one-hour weekly one-to-one telecollaborative language exchange sessions for eight weeks (see Table 6.2).

As illustrated in Table 6.2, the program was designed to ensure that learners could maintain ongoing interaction over the course of eight weeks, with progress monitored through two sessions where all participants convene. Everyday topics were selected to facilitate initial conversations, gradually progressing to more open-ended discussions. In light of the above, this project aimed to explore the development of L2 learners' interactional competence and intercultural awareness, both of which were promoted through the proposed language exchange buddy system. This study seeks to address two key research questions:

- How do second language learners (English and Japanese language learners) at the post-elementary level develop their interactional competence (the ability to participate in conversation in their target language, maintain conversation, and repair interactional problems) through language exchange programs?

TABLE 6.2 *Eight-Week Language and Culture Exchange Project Schedule*

Week	Activity (1 hour) 30 minutes for Japanese and English language	Topic of the week followed by free talk
W1	Meeting with everyone	Introductory session, 15 minutes rotations at first encounters
W2	One-on-one session	Detailed self-introduction (e.g., college enrolment dates, major, hobby, what's special about your study, family members, etc.)
W3	One-on-one session	Food (likes/dislikes), favourite sports or athletes
W4	Meeting with everyone	Follow up sessions, introduction to use of fillers and topic-development, 15 minutes rotations with different partners discussing reason for study Japanese/English, what is easy or difficult to study
W5	One-on-one session	My university life (music, games, films, animes, favourite Japanese/British person)
W6	One-on-one session	Countries or cultures I am interested in
W7	One-on-one session	Part-time jobs I do, what I do exactly
W8	One-on-one session	Summer break plan, things I want to achieve by the end of the summer break

♦ What are the types of cultural awareness, that will be raised among L2 learners participating in the language exchange programs?

6.2.4.3 *Learners' Reflections on Communication in Intercultural Settings*

Drawing on the experiences gained from this project, as well as feedback from both learners and teacher-researchers, this section highlights how the project was perceived as an effective pedagogical practice for enhancing interactional and intercultural competence through online language and cultural exchanges.

Japanese language learners:

I definitely feel more confident about speaking in Japanese now. Or rather, I am confident that I am able to use it if necessary. I still would not consider myself 'confident,' but I think I would feel more able to initiate or maintain a conversation in Japanese in the future, as I have learned that I am able to do so through this project. (Student 2)

I was able to speak a lot about Bulgarian culture and I can now see similarities with Japanese culture. I am glad my partner was so interested, and we shared a lot of information. (Student 1)

English language learners:

I was able to relax while speaking throughout this project and it made me feel that I can maintain conversation, even if when is a bit longer. (Student 13)

I developed a positive attitude to trying to express my opinion even with mistakes, as my partner tried to understand. I became more confident when speaking in English, without being afraid of making mistakes. (Student 11)

I became aware of a wide range of unique expressions in Japanese, involving onomatopoeia or formulaic expressions. (Student 13).

6.2.4.4 Benefits Identified by Teacher-Researchers

As teacher-researchers who organized this pedagogical and research project, we believe that it now reflects our experiences of organizing this type of program from the perspective of L2 teachers in each language and also of researchers with expertise in the field of pragmatics and conversation analysis, sharing reflections on: (1) motivation and pedagogical benefits, (2) observation of learner engagement, (3) benefits of this program as a whole and (4) limitations and further pedagogical implications.

A Japanese Language Teacher:

As a convenor for a Japanese language module for the beginner, I had been thinking about opportunities for beginner level students to engage in natural interaction in their target language regularly and the effects of such pedagogical practice. As mentioned, I have been organizing the visitor sessions within classroom hours. While two sessions per year provide facilitating motivation and confidence in learners' interactional skills in initial natural encounters and opportunities for self-reflection on their use of L2, it is in its nature a one-off session which seeks regular base opportunities over several weeks. Based on overall observations of learner engagement, I witnessed many interesting topics which students learning English and Japanese can share with enthusiasm, but not necessarily with teachers in class, such as K-culture and K-pop related topics, games, animations, difficulties or enjoyment of L2 learning and university life. It was also a joy to see them share their own cultural interpretations of each other's food, sports, festivals and lifestyles, taking in their historical background and the ways they reflected their own cultures. As for future possibilities, it is for educators to explore how to support and bridge individual learners' valuable experiences and knowledge and the confidence they gained through this project, which can be further enriched in their classrooms, as they seek connections between classroom and real language use beyond discursive pedagogical applications. (Seiko)

English Language Teacher:

During my teaching of English language classes at colleges in Japan for the past several years, of which most focus on reading and essay writing, I have realized first-hand that these students display a fundamental problem: they are knowledgeable in terms of English grammar and vocabulary; however, most of them lack hands-on experience interacting with native English speakers. Hence, being unable to comprehend what is heard and provide their immediate responses, their overall communication skills in English are low. As described by the Japanese language teacher above, I too was searching for the opportunities for my students to authentically engage in natural conversation in English in a more private context. "Authentically" here implies the environment where they can be exposed to the "live" English spoken by the people of their generation, including some expressions in fashion and slang in their actual daily life. "Private context" means mostly the one-on-one interaction setting, where they feel easy to discuss their families, friends, life events, etc., without embarrassment. This was due to the nature of many of my Japanese students who were on the quiet side and did not possess the confidence or courage to speak up not only in English, but also even in Japanese in the classroom.

This project's English authenticity greatly differed from the slow-paced English that is catered to the students' level, using simple vocabulary and grammatical constructions, etc. This is the way many English conversation schools in Japan typically conduct their classes. The students' topics were also authentic, which included ones that were currently socially discussed and popular among their generation. Therefore, when my Japanese language learning colleague and I came up with this one-on-one buddy project, in which a British student engages in English conversation with a Japanese student for a certain period, then they switch to Japanese conversation, it seemed like a brilliant idea. Especially in the time of advanced technological tools being available, utilizing online video-talk applications such as Zoom and Google Classroom as an interactional platform, the students in the same generation on both ends can meet and casually interact with each other – this was a mutually beneficial, fun opportunity for the students (Junko).

Benefits, challenging aspects and future possibilities:

As mentioned, authenticity was the key benefit the students were supplied with in this program. These students were around 19-20 years old, and they seemed to enjoy sharing their similar interests and knowledge about each other's countries and pop cultures, which the college professors usually did not even know. I also recognized the students' efforts to have their partners comprehend what they were discussing by employing a great deal of gestures, facial expressions, pictures, and even showing their cell phones over the screen. They attempted to search for any common and sharable topics – exhibiting their willingness for alignment and building solidarity – which I believe is an extremely significant, basic skill when engaging in interaction with anyone.

Having said that, there were some challenges to be addressed. Since it was a one-on-one conversation, if the silence continued, there was some "awkward" ambience which appeared to make both or one of the partners uneasy. Because silence may be treated differently especially between the Western and Eastern interactional cultures, there may have been some sort of mismatch in their communication format. However, I consider this element as a part of the necessary learning process for intercultural communication, which implies that, for instance, a Japanese student should learn to not stay quiet while a British student may like to gain tolerance to such silence. This is just one example out of many different non-linguistic cross-cultural challenges.

In terms of future possibilities, based on what we observed from their interactions, this type of program may produce the most effective result if students are provided with pragmatic training courses that would include these differences prior to the program. We indeed attempted to teach the British side on how Japanese frequently use backchannels, "un" (yeah) "a, sou desu ka" (oh, is that so?) etc., as a default feature of listenership after the program began. It seems that the British students effectively used them when interacting in Japanese with their Japanese partners. Being students of a Japanese major in the U.K. and being students of an English major in Japan, they are regularly taught the basic linguistic elements such as grammar rules, pronunciation, and vocabulary, etc., to begin with. Intercultural communication, however, requires a lot more non-linguistic aspects that accompany the interaction itself. Thus, before initiating the buddy conversation-exchange program and practicing these elements, it is important that students be fully taught and become aware of the significance of these pragmatic factors (Junko).

Reflections from L2 learners illustrate how their confidence levels and attitudes to collaborative interaction were highly positive and encouraged them to take further steps following genuine reactions and support from their partners. Teacher-researchers also saw the benefits of this type of language programme, which can provide authentic interaction, enabling learners to talk about their mutual interests and exchange ideas based on their intercultural curiosity.

6.3 Cross-Cultural Encounters of English and Japanese Language Learners Studying Abroad

In this section, we learn from L2 learners' experiences during study abroad. Three English language learners, Nana (Finland, at her ninth month), Misuzu (Belgium, at her 2nd month), Yumika (UK, at her sixth month) and four Japanese language learners in Japan in their third to fourth month, Alfie, Mila, Natasja and Peter shared their study abroad experiences from intercultural perspectives, looking at: (1) aspirations for study abroad before departure; (2) differences between educational environments in their home and host countries; (3) difficulties experienced due to cross-cultural differences and the use of English or Japanese as L2, and (4) invaluable experiences gained through study abroad. Japanese learners of English shared their reflections in Japanese, prior to translation by the author.

6.3.1 English Language Learners

Nana:

> As for academic aspects, I found out that in Finland, self-initiated participation was encouraged while in Japan, we usually listen to the lectures passively. In Finland, all classes had

only 20 to 30 students, so sharing individual opinions was encouraged. I had a great opportunity to research Japan, making comparisons to other countries. That brought me valuable opportunities to learn about both the positive and negative aspects of Japan. Most exchange students in Finland were from other European countries. There were students who were interested in Japan, which is far away from Europe but there were also others who spoke about Japan from stereotypical perspectives. I spent a lot of time with my roommate, another exchange student who wasn't Japanese. As we both communicated in the second language, there were occasions when we misunderstood each other, and I gradually felt we were tired of spending all our time together. However, as I explained my culture and lifestyle, she came to understand my values, attitudes, and behavior and respected my free time. I learned the importance of trying to communicate with my broken English. There were occasions when I found it hard to face direct criticism or honest opinions, but I also found that experience new and interesting. By expressing yourself openly, you can get closer, and I also found myself cherishing my way of living. I was busy when I was in Japan, so I found myself struggling to decide how to use my time in Finland as I could not do very much during wintertime, which led me to feel its lifestyle was boring. However, I was impressed by the idea that you should 'cherish what you have and enjoy the time you don't have' and started hiking or going to the gym, finding ways to enjoy myself without spending money. Although my pride in my English proficiency, which was highly praised in Japan, was shattered when I tried to speak English in Finland, this led me to stop talking sometimes. However, observing my roommate trying to communicate and initiate interaction motivated me to try again. Every time I faced difficulties; I had to discuss them with my friends. At these times, we did not force each other to accept our own cultures or ways of thinking but understood each other's culture and adopted a new way of living which helped each of us to build a good rapport, cherishing our friendship as well. My friend was very interested in her country's politics, and this reminded me of my lack of knowledge of Japan. Studying abroad gave me the opportunity to get to know others from different countries, but also enabled me to abandon stereotyped perspectives and prejudices when conversing with others, as we tried to see the world through each other's experiences instead. This transformed me into a person, able to be honest about myself and towards others. My ten-month study abroad experience was extremely fruitful (Nana, an exchange student in Finland, original reflection in Japanese).

Nana's study abroad experience provided invaluable opportunities for her to learn more about language and culture, her own way of thinking, as well as her attitudes toward herself and others, seen through the lens of a global perspective. Her struggles in intercultural communication with other international students led her to face new challenges and this helped her to develop a fresh perspective on intercultural communication.

Misuzu:

My aspiration before participating in study abroad was to improve my English proficiency and raise my intercultural awareness. Upon my arrival in Belgium, I was able to recognize cultural differences through daily life and communication or activities I shared with students from other countries. I often find it difficult to understand languages when I do shopping, ending up using Google Translate or asking shop assistants, as Belgium has three official languages: Dutch, French and German. Also, I felt uncomfortable being an in-between with people who have different communication styles, for example, those who share their opinions directly or those who prefer to do so implicitly. Also, lifestyles can differ across cultures, and I feel there are many occasions when I lose the rhythm of my accustomed lifestyle. But through these experiences, I learned it is important for me to accept cultural differences gradually and look at things around me holistically. There were times that I felt loneliness in a foreign country, which led me miss my family and friends in Japan. But at the same time, whenever

> *seeking to overcome these difficulties, I felt I was able to enrich my life gradually. Also, through intercultural communication, I was able to share various way of thinking, values and ways of life with people from different countries and I believe this will be my treasure in my future career and life* (Misuzu, a Japanese exchange student in Belgium, original in Japanese).

Misuzu's reflections highlight the interactional difficulties she faced while studying abroad in multilingual contexts. As she navigated the use of different languages, she also encountered various communication styles. However, she viewed these challenges as learning opportunities, which allowed her to enrich her ways of thinking and foresee long-term benefits for her future endeavors.

Yumika:

> *My aspiration before study abroad was to jump into new environments and acquire practical aptitude in the use of English. Reflecting on my experiences, I can see that in Japan I tended to hesitate before trying something. However much I wanted to try, I was too afraid of making mistakes. I was anxious about revealing myself as someone who can make mistakes and being judged by others. I therefore set myself the positive target of trying something new during my study abroad. Also, when communicating with my friends who are native English speakers, I struggled to use the English I had learned at school in Japan, along with the knowledge I had gained. I realized there were so many expressions I still did not know and really wanted to find ways I could use the knowledge obtained in my English classes and to learn expressions beyond school textbooks. That led me to set one of my goals. When I came to the UK, there were a lot of occasions when I worried that my English wouldn't get across what I wanted to say or might sound impolite. But my fried said 'I know you are trying to speak politely, so do not worry.' Her words made me relaxed and helped me to speak gradually. Of course, I am still careful about the way I talk, but in terms of communication, her words*

of encouragement were a major source of help. As for cultural differences, I felt that were so many occasions when you need to express your opinions more directly and this made me it difficult for me to express my intentions as I wished, or when I felt that I was told something with strong language. Conversely, often I am still concerned that expressions I use make others uncomfortable. These difficulties were greater than I imagined before beginning study abroad. Nevertheless, respecting others is the key ot intercultural communication. If you respect others' culture and language, it becomes natural for you to be able to accept others and my spoken English will improve in response to my strong motivation to express my opinions and feelings to others (Yumika, a Japanese exchange student in the UK, original in Japanese).

Yumika shared her positive attitudes and extensive efforts to try new approaches in the UK, which helped raise her confidence level throughout her study abroad experience. Her psychological shift toward more confident L2 use was facilitated by various intercultural communications with local people. Her self-reflection and discoveries emphasized the importance of respecting others' cultural values.

6.3.2 Japanese Language Learners

Four Japanese language learners from a British university shared their study abroad experiences related to communication in Japanese contexts, starting three months after their arrival. Alfie and Mila compared Japanese and British cultures, while Peter and Natasja discussed issues of social acceptance and invisible borders they encountered as learners of Japanese who sought to become part of new communities in Japan.

Alfie:

Before my study abroad experience, I felt pretty confident with my reading and writing ability as that's what we tested and practiced in class the most. I definitely lacked confidence when it came to speaking and holding a conversation because I didn't have time to think about and dissect the language structure the way I could when I was practicing reading comprehension for example. Therefore, a major aspiration of mine for the year abroad was to become more confident with speaking and having conversations in Japanese. Additionally, I felt pretty confident with the course content of second year, if anything I found it quite easy, so I was really looking forward to a challenge. In reality, I haven't encountered many difficulties in communicating with people here, and I think that's due in part to shared cultural values between the UK and Japan. I think it's an unpopular opinion, but I believe we have a lot in common, in terms of communication styles and otherwise. Both cultures value politeness and saving face highly. We will say what we think we should say, rather than what we truly believe. We both are often vague and beat around the bush. Despite English not having a clear distinction between polite and impolite speech the same way Japanese does, we are taught to use academic rhetoric in writing and such. The way we talk to those above us is very different to how we talk to our friends. The main difference is aizuchi which in the UK we don't do very much as we're taught being a good listener is to be quiet and focus on what the other person is saying. Whereas in Japan if you do that you come across as cold and disinterested. This has happened a few times in my experience, but I think a lot of Japanese people know foreigners don't use aizuchi as much as they do, so it's just a cultural difference in communication rather than us being cold and disinterested. Something I think that has developed my insights in communication with Japanese people is definitely the amount of conversing I do with them. I've become more accustomed to natural Japanese speech as a result of being so much more exposed to it than back home. Being able to replicate that and speak naturally has really provided an insight into communication as Japanese people speak to me in a way, they would any stranger, as opposed to a foreign tourist. I think my Japanese ability has massively aided that as in my experience, people seem to be instantly put at ease when you open your mouth and speak good Japanese. I think my Japanese has drastically improved in the few short months I've been here. Having

> so much input, and all my classes being entirely in Japanese has significantly improved my listening abilities as well as how quickly I can process information. The grammar covered in class has been advanced and allowed me to feel more conversational and able to understand more complex texts. Taking a class in book reading has improved my confidence in such a field such that now I am able to read Japanese novels in their originality, which I've found very rewarding. I feel comfortable in my command of the Japanese language and am able to navigate life here without so much as a hitch. I look forward to next semester where I will take even more challenging classes which will only see my ability grow even further.

Alfie's reflection illustrates the similarities between British and Japanese communication styles, particularly regarding the shared values of politeness and face-saving strategies. He also commented on the use of *aizuchi* (reactive tokens), which are notable characteristics of Japanese communication. Alfie's perspective on these differences stems from his unique, culturally diverse interactional resources. His positive attitude is evident in his determination and curiosity to explore new challenges.

Mila

> My aspirations before I left for Japan were to work on N3/N2 level of Japanese proficiency test (JLPT) in Japan so I can be ready to work at N2/N1 level in year 4. I had (and still have) aspirations to write Kanji and be able to express myself like a native speaker in both writing and speaking. I have goals of reading and listening in Japanese, being able to understand most things in most contexts. I also had very big aspirations on oral communication that I am trying to get closer to achieving day by day. I haven't experienced particular difficulties in communication due to cross-cultural differences. I believe that there has been common ground with everyone whom I have spoken to. The difficulties for me are mostly ones of not being sure how to express myself in a way that is also true to my personality as well as grammatically

> correct. I believe that the more I speak, the less of a difficulty I experience. I try to copy patterns of speech that I like, and I identify myself with and mimic phrases that I like, trying to adopt them in my speech. However, I have not experienced an intense Japanese-only environment outside of my classes where the teachers only speak Japanese. Despite this, I have been in many situations such as going to the post office or in some stores, where I have to conduct everything in Japanese without any external help, which has been successful so far. I recently signed up for language exchange at my university in Japan and I am looking forward as this program is described to be stricter on outcomes. I am very hopeful that I will be able to improve through my participation in it. As I mentioned above, I think that the more I speak the more confident I feel as I try to adopt the speaking style that suits me. We speak a lot in the classes here and I find that I speak better when I am asked a particular question. From that question I can extend my thoughts in Japanese and form a conversation. I am taking a class that covers verbal communication in casual and formal settings. I feel a struggle in that class that is related to not knowing exactly how to say something which stops me from saying anything at all. To overcome this, I talk to my friends in class, and we figure out together an appropriate response rather than relying on a definite answer given by the teachers. It makes me feel like I am truly using the language and extending the use of it for myself.

Mila's reflection also highlights the commonalities in the communication styles of British and Japanese cultures, rather than focusing on differences. However, she expresses a desire to immerse herself in Japanese-only contexts in Japan, indicating that it is not always easy for exchange students to find such opportunities during their study abroad. Furthermore, her experiences with using both casual and formal Japanese demonstrate her determination and curiosity to develop her own way of expressing herself with her friends, rather than simply accepting predefined answers as an L2 user.

Social acceptance towards my L2 learning:

Natasja

> One of the main struggles I have experienced on my year abroad has been facing other people's opinions about the value of learning Japanese. These opinions come not only from Western friends but also from teachers and Japanese people. For example, I was recently told by a non-Japanese member of staff at my university, that becoming completely fluent in Japanese is not beneficial as a foreigner in Japan. They suggested that by being a foreigner, and by acting like one to some extent, Japanese people will make allowances for culturally inappropriate behavior because foreigners are held to a lower standard than Japanese people. Foreigners are not expected to understand the Japanese way of life whereas fluent Japanese speakers are held to a higher standard, which may make life harder. Another example is that people often express surprise and confusion when I tell them I am a Japanese language student. It seems that some people do not consider the study of Japanese to be useful. Encountering such attitudes has been discouraging at times because learning Japanese is challenging, and it is disheartening to hear that your efforts are not valued. However, this is not to say that all reactions towards my Japanese study have been negative. There have also been interactions where a Japanese speaker has been relieved that I can communicate with them in Japanese. Often, I have found that Japanese people appreciate when foreigners attempt to use Japanese rather than immediately resort to English. Overall, I think that people questioning my reasons for learning Japanese has encouraged me to consider this question more deeply. Facing a certain level of disapproval regarding my pursuit of Japanese language learning, has forced me to develop self-assurance. It has me to validate my own choices rather than relying on the approval of members of society. Furthermore, it makes me feel extremely grateful that I am free to choose what path I want to take in life, regardless of others' opinions.

> *In terms of language study, I have found that my Japanese language learning trajectory at university differed from my previous study of European languages in school. When learning Spanish and German, I felt that my progress was steady and consistent. However, when studying Japanese, I have found that my progress plateaus and is followed by a perceived 'breakthrough moment', rather than a slow and steady increase in ability. For large periods, although I was consistent in my language study, I felt that my progress was stagnating and that my Japanese was not improving. This would then be followed by a moment of realization where I would feel like I had made sudden progress. For example, during the interview for my year abroad Japanese language placement test, I felt like my speaking ability had suddenly improved. After the interview, I even became concerned that this seemingly sudden improvement was temporary and that I would not be able to replicate that level of speaking in class. Of course, this improvement was a result of the consistent practice that came before the interview, but it did not feel that way in the moment. Other examples include being able to understand train announcements for the first time, becoming able to read supermarket labels and understanding the kanji on adverts. Overall, I have experienced progress in Japanese in small bursts between extended periods of effort with no perceived reward. Having now completed this cycle a few times, it has been reassuring to remind myself in periods of perceived stagnation, that the next breakthrough must be approaching.*

Natasja shared valuable reflections on some Japanese people's reactions to her positive evaluation of learning Japanese, which was truly disheartening. These reactions highlighted an invisible, pre-determined boundary between being Japanese or non-Japanese. However, Natasja later reframed this experience positively, using it as an opportunity for self-reflection and searching for her own answers as a user of the Japanese language. Her determination is clearly depicted as a sign of agency in her discursive practice. Additionally, her observation of her learning process as a multilingual learner highlights an interesting journey that differs from her experience of learning European languages. While being unable to see steady improvement can be challenging, her curiosity about new ways to improve her Japanese remains strikingly positive.

Peter:

Before I began my study abroad, I was quite conscious that I was weaker in speaking ability relative to the other three core language skills of listening, reading, and writing. My main goal for the study abroad period has thus been to try to bolster my speaking ability and bring it to the same level as my language ability in other areas. Of course, it goes without saying that I aim to improve in all areas, but I feel that having such a disparity with one aspect of my language ability has a strongly negative impact on my overall language proficiency, which I hope through my study abroad experience to rectify.

One of the main issues with language usage I have encountered during my first three months in Japan has been with highly formal or regimented speech in everyday situations. While I understand such language in theory, I have encountered it much more often in everyday life than I had expected. For example, during my first few weeks, I often struggled to understand the cashiers in convenience stores and supermarkets, as they would ask fairly basic questions in – from an outside perspective – unnecessarily complicated Japanese. Instead of 'do you need a bag?' or 'do you have a points card?', I would instead hear things like 'how about a cashier bag with your purchase?' or 'are you the holder of a points card with our store?'. While I have now grown accustomed to the 'routine' of which questions are asked, I still regularly find myself unable to fully process the grammar or sentence structure of the highly rehearsed and systematized language used by service staff and usually answer based on instinct or a single keyword.

Through my interactions with Japanese people since I have been here, I have become very familiar with a feeling

> akin to crossing a 'boundary' or 'filter' when conversing with a Japanese person. In my experiences thus far, Japanese people come across generally guarded when initiating conversation but given the right context or upon recognition that I can speak some Japanese, there is often, to me, a very apparent lowering of this guard. For example, cashiers often have a look of mild concern when I approach the counter, but I have sometimes observed a visible relaxation when I say something in Japanese to them (like 'can I also have a bag, please' or 'I have a points card').
>
> I also noticed this same 'boundary' or 'filter' at the recent student festival at my host university. While the occasional brief interactions I have had with Japanese students around the campus since I have been in Japan have invariably been awkward and stiff, everyone at the festival was extremely relaxed and willing to speak freely with me. Maybe I am mistaken, but I got the strong impression that everyone I spoke to would generally behave as they did on this day if not for societal decorum dictating that they act more restrained in everyday life. It is my impression that when presented with an occasion like the student festival where everyone is under the same understanding of what sort of atmosphere is desired, people felt freely able to be themselves without having to filter their thoughts through a mask of propriety. I am still very keenly aware of my weak speaking ability, but it is comforting to know that I am clearly making some progress as evidenced by the experiences outlined above.

Peter's reflections on his new experience communicating with service staff at Japanese supermarkets highlight his unexpected encounter with unfamiliar and highly routinized expressions. This illustrates the difference between language learned in class and its use in authentic social contexts. While these experiences remain somewhat of a curiosity for Peter at times, his attempts to respond to such questions, coupled with his continuous observation in these settings, may encourage him to explore new perspectives on these systematized expressions in Japanese contexts. In contrast, his observations of Japanese students' attitudes and communication during a school festival gave him an opportunity to experience a situation where rituals and social barriers were lowered. Peter's reflections on the moment when Japanese people opened up upon discovering he could communicate in Japanese further demonstrate how social boundaries can diminish.

6.4 Reflections on L2 Learners' Study Abroad Experiences

The valuable insights shared by English language learners studying in European countries and Japanese language learners in Japan suggest that, during the initial stage of their study abroad, international students encounter circumstances that are both unexpected and unfamiliar from linguistic and cultural perspectives. They find themselves in a new community and explore ways to exercise agency in their use of the L2 when communicating with local people, classmates, and teachers. While their psychological struggles can hinder their confidence in intercultural interactions, their reflections highlight how these struggles can serve as a springboard for further self-reflection, allowing them to refresh their perspectives and learn from the social contexts in which they are situated. Although individual learners take diverse approaches to developing their interactional and cultural repertoires, their reflections demonstrate how study abroad experiences can be a powerful catalyst for their future growth as L2 users.

6.4.1 Practical Approaches to Promoting Intercultural Communication on Campus

During their initial transition into university life, international students often encounter a range of challenges that affect their well-being and hinder their ability to adapt. These challenges include language barriers, cultural adjustment, academic stress, financial difficulties, isolation and loneliness, and homesickness. Such difficulties may impede students' integration into their new environment and hinder their academic and social success. In this section, we aim to offer practical suggestions to enhance the sense of belonging of international students while also promoting intercultural interactions between domestic and international students.

6.4.2 Cultural Immersion Events

Cultural immersion events are designed to expose students to a wide range of cultures to foster intercultural interactions on campus. These events go beyond simply learning about a culture through lectures or textbooks. Instead, they offer an opportunity for students to experience and interact with elements of a culture that can lead to deeper understanding, appreciation, and connection. Soyhan offers practical recommendations aimed at fostering intercultural exchange between domestic and international students on a Filipino university campus:

> *To foster global awareness and cross-cultural competencies, our short-term study abroad program combines five weeks of English language instruction with project-based learning. Students can choose from a range of destinations each year, including the Philippines, Malaysia, and Canada. During their stay, students study English and visit various sites to identify local issues and work on projects to provide solutions. This year, I had the opportunity to chaperone a group of students during their study abroad program at a university on Cebu Island in the Philippines. One key difference between the Filipino program and the other programs is that, due to cultural and safety reasons, it is nearly impossible to arrange homestays for our students in the Philippines. As a result, students stay in a hotel during their five-week study abroad program. This limitation naturally reduces their opportunities for intercultural contact, as they don't have the chance to interact with host family members. Therefore, we needed to come up with practical solutions to enhance the intercultural exchange between our students and local students on campus. One such idea was to hold a small-scale Matsuri (Japanese word for the festival) on campus where domestic students could participate in activities with Japanese students, such as Shodo (Calligraphy), Origami (Paper Folding), and Japanese tea ceremony. This not*

only enhanced intercultural contact between our students and the domestic students but also showed our students that true intercultural interactions are mutual, where one can be both a recipient and, at times, a giver. This was an empowering process for both groups. While domestic students engaged in intercultural contact, which sparked their curiosity, they then researched more about these cultural artifacts, expanding their cross-cultural knowledge, it also raised our students' confidence in themselves, as they realized they could lead an activity and teach domestic students new things, despite being at a disadvantage in terms of language skills.

6.4.3 Intercultural Workshops

Another effective way to boost intercultural interactions on campus is by organizing intercultural workshops for students. These workshops offer a unique opportunity for students to engage with diverse cultural perspectives and raise awareness of cultural differences and similarities. This, in turn, helps students grasp the subtleties of communication styles, values, and social norms across cultures. Moreover, due to the interactive nature of these workshops, students can discuss real-world intercultural issues, such as cultural biases and stereotypes. By engaging in discussions about real-world intercultural issues, we can give students an opportunity to reflect on their own biases and assumptions. Reflective practice, combined with exposure to diverse perspectives, allows them to better understand the experiences and viewpoints of others. As a result, they develop greater empathy—meaning they can relate to and appreciate the feelings and experiences of people from different cultures. This deeper understanding helps break down stereotypes, promotes open-mindedness, and fosters a more inclusive, respectful attitude toward others (Egitim, 2024b; Farrell, 2022; Sowa, 2009). Soyhan illustrates this point with an example from one of the intercultural workshops he regularly organizes:

> *In one of the workshops, we regularly organize, the speaker used storytelling to challenge presumptions. He shared a story about*

an encounter between him and his colleague who was organizing a trip for his students to a famous tourist site in Kyoto, Japan where students would be tasked with initiating conversations with foreigners. The speaker and I divided our students into groups where they reflected on what was potentially wrong with the idea of the speaker's colleague who had asked his students to initiate conversations with foreigners. In each group, we intentionally placed both international and domestic students. Later, we invited one student from each group to offer their perspective. We were all surprised by the diversity of perspectives we heard from the students. One student mentioned that initiating conversations with foreigners could feel forced or uncomfortable, while another student emphasized that such an approach might assume all foreigners share the same characteristics or interests, which can lead to stereotypes. In the end, we raised the question: how do we identify who is a foreigner? At that moment, the classroom fell silent as everyone realized that it would be nearly impossible to identify who was a foreigner without making assumptions based on appearance. While some Asians may be foreigners, there are also third-culture or mixed-race individuals who identify as Japanese. This activity proved to be a great experience for students to view issues beyond their horizon and challenge their assumptions about identity, fostering a deeper understanding of the complexities of culture and belonging. When these workshops are held on a regular basis, students are encouraged to challenge stereotypes, cultivate open-mindedness, and develop a more inclusive and respectful attitude toward others.

6.4.4 Intercultural Sports Day

The benefit of an Intercultural Sports Day on campus in promoting intercultural communication lies in its ability to bring together individuals from diverse cultural backgrounds in a shared, interactive experience. Through teamwork, friendly competition, and physical activity, participants have the opportunity to dismantle cultural barriers, enhance mutual understanding, and cultivate respect for one another's beliefs, values, and communication styles. Moreover, an Intercultural Sports Day offers a practical platform for students to engage in cross-cultural exchanges, thereby contributing to the enhancement of intercultural dialogue. One example is where domestic and international students are divided into mixed teams and participate in relay races. During the races, each team member is responsible for completing a different cultural activity, such as performing a dance from their home country or answering trivia questions about each other's cultures. Since each team member brings unique skills and cultural knowledge to the table, communication, coordination, and mutual support are required to win the competition. Therefore, students have no choice but to rely on one another to complete the various cultural activities successfully. Sports demonstrations can also provide opportunities for both domestic and international students to learn and practice together. For instance, in a martial arts demonstration, students can share their knowledge and techniques, fostering mutual respect and appreciation by allowing students to share and learn from each other's cultural practices, when students from diverse backgrounds demonstrate martial arts techniques or traditional movements, they not only teach their peers about their culture but also gain insight into the discipline and values that underpin these practices. This exchange creates an environment of respect as participants learn to appreciate the depth and significance of different traditions while building teamwork and communication skills. Peer mentorship or role modeling plays a crucial role in guiding this process, ensuring that cultural exchange is both constructive and mutually enriching (Hooper et al., 2025; Wong et al., 2022). Needless to say, these principles apply to various types of sports and activities where participants engage with different cultural practices, learn from one another's traditions, and develop mutual respect.

All in all, promoting intercultural communication on campus is essential for fostering an inclusive, respectful, and globally aware academic environment. Through cultural immersion events, intercultural workshops, and activities such as an Intercultural Sports Day, universities can create opportunities for both domestic and international students to engage with diverse cultures, challenge stereotypes, and develop a deeper understanding of one another. These initiatives not only enhance students' intercultural competence but also encourage mutual respect and appreciation for different cultural practices and values. By regularly facilitating these interactions, institutions can help students build the skills needed to navigate an increasingly interconnected world, contributing to their academic success, personal growth, and the overall harmony of the campus community (Fuentes et al., 2021).

6.5 Conclusion

In this chapter, we have explored the multifaceted dimensions of study abroad experiences and tandem learning, particularly focusing on East Asian learners, with an emphasis on promoting intercultural interactions between domestic and international students. Through a comparison of face-to-face and online visitor sessions, we have highlighted the pedagogical frameworks and procedures that shape intercultural interactions in global learning environments. Learners' voices and their perspectives offer valuable insights into what is learned in terms of communication within intercultural contexts, emphasizing the importance of practical engagement in *global competence* development. We have identified various benefits and challenges, through the experiences of learners, volunteers, and teacher-researchers while also underscoring the evolving nature of intercultural communication and the need for adaptable teaching strategies.

As demonstrated through initiatives such as cultural immersion events, intercultural workshops, and sports days, practical approaches to fostering intercultural interactions on university campuses can play an important role in both academic and extracurricular settings. These initiatives not only promote intercultural exchange but also prepare learners to navigate diverse global contexts with increased sensitivity, awareness, and flexibility. Moving forward, continued research and innovation in these areas will be key to refining strategies that equip students with the skills needed for successful communication and collaboration in an increasingly globalized world.

References

Akiyama, Y. (2017). Vicious vs. virtuous cycles of turn negotiation in American-Japanese telecollaboration: Is silence a virtue? *Language and Intercultural Communication*, *17*(2), 190–209. https://doi.org/10.1080/14708477.2016.1277231

Aubrey, S. (2017). Measuring Flow in the EFL classroom: Learners' perception of Inter- and Intra-cultural task-based interaction. *TESOL Quarterly*, *51*(3), 661–692. https://doi.org/10.1002/tesq.387

Bao, D. (2019). English in the real world: What classroom pedagogy has not taught. *Transitions: Journal of Transient Migration*, *3*(2), 109–126. https://doi.org/10.1386/tjtm_00002_1

Beelen, J., & Jones, E. (2015). Redefining internationalization at home. In A. Curaj, L. Latei, R. Pricopie, J. Salmi, & P. Scott (Eds.), *The European higher education area: Between critical reflections and future policies* (pp. 59–72). https://doi.org/10.1007/978-3-319-20877-0_5

Bruce, B., & Newman, D. (1978). Interacting plans. Centre for the study of reading, Report #88, Cambridge, Mass,: Bolt, Beranek and Newman, Inc.

Burden, P. (2020). Do Japanese university students want to study abroad? *The Language Teacher*, *44*(2), 3–11.

Byram, M. (1997). *Teaching and assessing intercultural communication competence*. Multilingual Matters.

Byram, M. (2009). The intercultural speaker and the pedagogy of foreign language education. In D. Deardorff (Ed.), *The SAGE handbook of intercultural competence* (pp. 321–332). Sage. https://doi.org/10.4135/9781071872987.n18

Carnals, L. (2024). Lost in translation: Intercultural understanding in oral interaction in an e-tandem virtual exchange. *Language and Intercultural Communication*, 1–15. https://doi.org/10.1080/14708477.2023.2298902

Chen, A. S. Y., Wu, I. H., & Bian, M. D. (2014). The moderating effects of active and agreeable conflict management styles on cultural intelligence and cross-cultural adjustment. *International Journal* of *Cross-Cultural Management, 14*(3), 270–288. https://doi.org/10.1177/1470595814525064

Deardorff, D. K. (2006). Identification and assessment of intercultural competence as a student outcome of internationalization. *Journal of Studies in International Education, 10*(3), 241–266. https://doi.org/10.1177/1028315306287002

Egitim, S. (2022). *Collaborative leadership through leaderful classroom practices: Everybodyis a leader.* Candlin & Mynard e-publishing. https://doi.org/10.47908/22

Egitim, S., & Uemiya, Y. (2023). *Leaderful classroom pedagogy through an interdisciplinary lens: Merging theory with practice.* Springer Nature.

Egitim, S. & Umemiya, Y. (2023). Leaderful classroom pedagogy through a multidisciplinary lens: Merging theory with practice. Springer Nature. https://doi.org/10.1007/978-981-99-6655-4

Egitim, S. (2024a). Does language teachers' intercultural competence influence oral participation in EFL classrooms?: Unveiling learner perspectives through a mixed methods inquiry. *Journal of Multilingual and Multicultural Development,* 1–34. https://doi.org/10.1080/01434632.2024.2306169

Egitim, S. (2024b). Voices on language teacher stereotypes: Critical cultural competence building as a pedagogical strategy. *Journal of Language, Identity, & Education, 23*(6), 1–32. https://doi.org/10.1080/15348458.2022.2070847

Egitim, S. (2024). Does Language Teachers' Intercultural Competence Influence Oral Participation in EFL Classrooms?: Unveiling Learner Perspectives Through a Mixed Methods Inquiry. Journal of Multilingual and Multicultural Development, 1–34. Taylor & Francis. https://doi.org/10.1080/01434632.2024.2306169.

Erduyan, I., & Bozer, E. M. (2022). Ideological becoming through study abroad: Multilingual Japanese students in Turkey. *Linguistics and Education, 71,* 1–14. https://doi.org/10.1016/j.linged.2022.101062

Fantini, A. E. (2018). *Intercultural communicative competence in educational exchange: A multinational perspective.* Routledge. https://doi.org/10.4324/9781351251747

Farrell, T. S. (2022). *Reflective practice in language teaching.* Cambridge University Press. https://doi.org/10.1002/9781118784235.eelt0873

Fuentes, M. A., Zelaya, D. G., & Madsen, J. W. (2021). Rethinking the course syllabus: Considerations for promoting equity, diversity, and inclusion. *Teaching of Psychology*, *48*(1), 69–79. https://doi.org/10.1177/0098628320959979

Fukada, Y. (2017). A language learner's target language-mediated socializing in an affinity space in the host country: An autoethnography, *Study Abroad Research in Second Language Acquisition and International Education*, *2*(1), 53–79. https://doi.org/10.1075/sar.2.1.03fuk

Halenko, N., & Economidou-Kogetsidis, M. (2022). Japanese learners' spoken requests in the study abroad context: Appropriateness, speech rate and response time. *The Language Learning Journal*, *50*(4), 506–520. https://doi.org/10.1080/09571736.2022.2088441

Hall, K., Hellermann, J.., and Pekarek Doehler, S. (2011). L2 interactional competence and development. Multilingual Matters

Hamada, I., & Iwasaki, S. (2024). Assessing benefits: A comparative evaluation of English Japanese online intercultural exchanges (OIE) before and during the COVID-19 pandemic. *The Language Learning Journal*, *52*(5), 487–505. https://doi.org/10.1080/09571736.2024.2369920

Harumi, S. (2023a). Classroom silence and learner-initiated repair: Using conversation analysis-informed material design to develop interactional repertoires, *TESOL Journal*, *14*(1), e704.

Harumi, S. (2023b). The mediative role of learning materials: Raising L2 learners' awareness of silence and conversational repair during L2 interaction. *Journal of Silence Studies in Education*, *2*(2), 145–162. http://dx.doi.org/10.31763/jsse.v2i2.79

Harumi, S., & Takahashi, J. (2025). Collaborative Intercultural talk: *Japanese students' eTandem learning*. [Manuscript submitted for publication].

Hooper, D., Eyitim, S., & Hofhuis, J. (2025). Exploring the impact of near-peer role modeling on learners' basic psychological needs: Insights from English Classes in Japanese Higher Education. *International Journal of Educational Research Open*, *8*(1), 1–12. https://doi.org/10.1016/j.ijedro.2024.100429

Humphries, S., Aubrey, S., & King, J. (2023). Fluctuations in Japanese English majors' capacity to speak before, during, and after studying abroad, *System*, *113*, 1–13. https://doi.org/10.1016/j.system.2023.103001

Ikeda, R. (2020). Learning outcomes and self-perceived changes among Japanese university students studying English in the Philippines. *TESL-EJ*, *23*(4). https://tesl-ej.org/pdf/ej92/a1.pdf

Kachru, B. (1986). *The alchemy of English: The spread, function, and models in nonnative English*. Oxford University Press.

Kariya, T. (2024). A long & wrong road to globalization: Why have Japanese universities failed in "Catching up" in the twenty-first century? *Daedalus, 153*(2), 120–135. https://doi.org/10.1162/daed_a_02069

Kasper, G., & Kim, Y. (2015). Conversation-for-learning: Institutional talk beyond the classroom. In N. Markee (Ed.), *The Handbook of classroom discourse and interaction* (pp. 390–408). Wiley. https://doi.org/10.1002/9781118531242

Kelly, R., & Imamura, Y. (2024). Learner beliefs and Japanese exchange students at a Finnish university. In A. Károly, M. Kokkonen, M. Gerlander, & P. Taalas (Eds.), *Driving and embracing change: Learning and teaching languages and communication in higher education*. University of Jyváskylá. https://edition.fi/jyu/catalog/download/1127/1137/4296-1?inline=1

Kimura, D. (2019). "Seriously, I came here to study English": A narrative case study of a Japanese exchange student in Thailand. *Study Abroad Research in Second Language Acquisition and International Education, 4*(1), 70–95. https://doi.org/10.1075/sar.17020.kim

Kireeti, K., Egitim, S., & Thomson, B. J. (2024). Utilizing peer evaluation as a collaborative learning tool: Fostering autonomy satisfaction in English presentation classes. *Language Learning in Higher Education, 14*(2), 379–400. https://doi.org/10.1515/cercles-2024-0037

Kobayashi, Y. (2018). *The evolution of English language learners in Japan: Crossing Japan, The West, and South East Asia*. Routledge. https://doi.org/10.4324/9781315208749

Mann, S., & Walsh, S. (2017). *Reflective practice in English language teaching: Research-based principles and practices*. Routledge. https://doi.org/10.4324/9781315733395

Nam, M. (2018). Study-abroad experiences of two South Korean undergraduate students in an English-speaking and a non-English-speaking country. *The Asia-Pacific Education Researcher, 27*, 177–185. https://doi.org/10.1007/s40299-018-0376-3

Nishino, T., & Nakatsugawa, M. (2020). 'Successful' participation in intercultural exchange: Tensions in American Japanese telecollaboration. *Language Learning & Technology, 24*(1), 154–168. www.lltjournal.org/item/10125-44714/

Sabban-Taylor, A. (2021). Intercultural competence in a face-to-face tandem learning: A micro-analytic perspective. *Language and Intercultural Communication*, *21*(2), 304–317. https://doi.org/10.1080/14708477.2020.1837149

Siegel, A. (2022). Study abroad in Sweden: Japanese exchange students' perspectives of language use in University EMI courses. *Languages*, *7*(1), 3. https://doi.org/10.3390/languages7010003

Sowa, P. A. (2009). Understanding our learners and developing reflective practice: Conducting action research with English language learners. *Teaching and Teacher Education*, *25*(8), 1026–1032. https://doi.org/10.1016/j.tate.2009.04.008

Umino, T. (2023). Reconceptualizing the silent period: Stories of Japanese students studying abroad. *Journal of Silence Studies in Education*, *2*(2), 68–81. http://dx.doi.org/10.31763/jsse.v2i2.32

Varonis, E. M., & Gass, S. (1985). Miscommunication in native/nonnative conversation. *Language in Society*, *14*(3), 327–343. https://doi.org/10.1017/S0047404500011295

Warchulski, D.,& Ward, A. (2022). The effects of time spent abroad on Japanese EFL student engagement with language outside the classroom. *Kansei Gakuin University Humanities Review*, *27*, 33–44.

Wong, S. P., Soh, S. B., & Wong, M. L. L. (2022). Intercultural mentoring among university students: The importance of meaningful communication. *International Journal of Intercultural Relations*, *91*, 13–26. https://doi.org/10.1016/j.ijintrel.2022.08.008

Index

acknowledge differences through reflection 96
add new values to your intercultural repertoire 96
adopting values beyond our horizon framework 97
Aizuchi (back-channelling) 79, 112–14, 127, 145, 150–2, 174–5
Asia-Pacific region 3, 5, 19, 30–2, 69, 78, 80–1
assertive communication 67, 69, 73–5, 81

balancing cultural identity and newly acquired values 98–101
Basic Psychological Needs Framework 51
basic psychological needs (BPNs) 51–2
Bennett's Developmental Model of Intercultural Sensitivity (DMIS) 12–13
Byram's Intercultural Speaker Model 10–11

cognitive flexibility 11, 21, 68, 70, 72, 75, 81
Collaborative Online Intercultural Learning (COIL) 134, 138
colonial era impacts 90
Common European Framework of Reference (CEFR) 54
communication style adaptation 100
communication styles (direct *vs.* indirect/implicit *vs.* assertive) 16, 18–19, 66–81, 89
community and collective influences 99
Confucian-heritage education 15, 29
Confucian norms 6, 19, 67–8
conflict resolution strategy 100
conflict-resolution dynamics 93–5

conversation-analytic approach 54
conversational repair 54–5
conversational silence 35–8, 50–1, 54–5
cross-cultural encounters 67, 69, 72, 74, 78, 81
cultural adaptation 67, 70, 94–5, 99–101
cultural fluidity 86–7
cultural identity 87, 97–9
cultural transmission 98–9

Deardorff's Process Model 8, 11–12
discourse completion tasks 53

English as a Lingua Franca (ELF) 5, 9, 11, 29, 43, 134
English as World Language (EWL) 7, 13–14, 29, 31, 46–7, 53
ethnocentrism 87–9
ethnographers (students as) 44–5, 57
eye contact 68–9, 71–3

family influences 98
fillers 37, 54, 79, 110–12, 121, 135, 144–5, 147, 150, 152, 160, 164
Four-Step Framework 1, 14

global competence 1–3, 5, 7, 14–16, 20–1, 66, 75
Global Jinzai 5–7, 14

hand gestures 18–19, 69, 73–5, 79
high-context cultures/communication 50, 89
Honne and Tatemae (true feelings *vs.* public facade) 20–1, 95

impact of conflict on intercultural relationships 91–3
implicit communication 67, 71–4, 77, 79–81